COLD CALLING TECHNIQUES
(That Really Work!)

COLD CALLING TECHNIQUES
(That Really Work!)

Stephan Schiffman

Published by Adams Media Corporation
260 Center Street, Holbrook, MA 02343

ISBN: 1-55850-860-0

Printed in the United States of America

G   H   I   J

COVER PHOTOGRAPH: Dario Perla

REAR COVER PHOTOGRAPH: The Ira Rosen Studio, South Bellmore, NY

*This book is available at quantity discounts for bulk purchases.
For information, call 1-800-872-5627.*

Visit our home page at http://www.adamsonline.com

ACKNOWLEDGMENTS

Special thanks for help in preparing this book go to Avi Feinglass, whose help in developing the initial chapters was invaluable; to Marcela Deauna, who faithfully typed and retyped the manuscript and offered encouragement throughout; and especially to Brandon Toropov, who took the bare material and molded it into the work that it is. Finally, I offer a word of hope and thanks to the thousands of salespeople who, every day, bravely pick up the phone to face a barrage of "no thank you's," "don't call me again's," and just plain "not interested's" in the course of their cold calls. To these men and women, who indirectly contributed so much over the years to the formation of this book, I owe the greatest debt.

This book is dedicated to AFS.

CONTENTS

Introduction

Chapter 1
The One Successful Way to Call 15

Chapter 2
Getting an Appointment 29

Chapter 3
Handling Objections 45

Chapter 4
The Ledge System for Rescuing "Lost" Calls 59

Chapter 5
Reaching Your Decision Maker 69

Chapter 6
Soft Selling: Persistence and Enthusiasm 75

Chapter 7

Closing Sales Over the Phone 85

Chapter 8

"How'm I Doing?" 99

Chapter 9

The Perils of Reinventing the Wheel 111

Chapter 10

Business as War 121

Conclusion

The Lemonade Stand 129

APPENDIX: Sample Scripts..137

A Guarantee—and Some Straight Talk about Selling

This book and the techniques it outlines are guaranteed to work for you in obtaining more sales appointments over the phone. If they do not, we will gladly refund your full purchase price if you supply us with: a record of all telephone calls; and the scripts you've developed in accordance with the methods outlined in later chapters.

If, for any reason, you should have any problems concerning the book, please write me, Stephan Schiffman, c/o Bob Adams, Inc., 260 Center Street, Holbrook, Massachusetts, 02343.

❑   ❑   ❑   ❑

Whether you've been selling for many years, have just entered the world of sales, or are reading about it here for the first time, you must know one thing. There are some things about selling that make it tough.

The first, without a doubt, is rejection.

The second is the fact that you have to *continue* to sell—every single day. You can't skip a day. And you don't get paid if you take time off.

Of course, you know that the odds are against you. When you start selling, you are going to expect to get rejected. But the rejections are going to mean a lot more than you think.

For every twenty calls you make, you might end up seeing five people. If you're lucky. But for every five people you see, you're only going to make one sale. It doesn't take too much calculation to figure out that you'll end up with nineteen "no's."

So nineteen people are going to say "no" to you before you make a sale. There isn't another job in the world with odds like that.

Let's take a look at a baseball player. He might get up to bat four times and miss three balls, but if he gets up to bat and hits that fourth ball, he's hitting .250. Not bad. You don't even get close to that.

Watch your favorite sports professionals; you'll realize that your odds are probably a lot worse than theirs.

So what am I saying about selling? I'm saying it's not easy. It's something that, in order to do correctly, you must do on an ongoing basis. Day in. Day out.

But everything's not so bleak. After all, this book is about success, not failure. And believe me, you can succeed—like nobody's business—in the world of sales.

So let's start in by looking at the first tip that can turn you into a cold calling star. Let's look at the very beginning of your day.

When you hit the office in the morning, what's the first thing you do? Perhaps you open up that bag you got from the coffee shop and take out a cup of coffee and a doughnut or a bagel. You sit back, stare at the phone, then look away. A couple of minutes go by as you munch away and maybe leaf through a newspaper.

Last sip of coffee. Last bit of doughnut. You toss the paper cup and wrapper in the trash and close the newspaper. Then, right around 9:01, you pick up the telephone and make your first call. And your first mistake.

What was it? To find out, turn to Chapter One.

The One Successful Way to Call

Before beginning, I'd like to offer some rules that will help you in using this book. If you follow them, I guarantee you'll see results in your sales work. The rules aren't complicated at all. They are:

1. Finish the book before you do anything.

2. Don't close yourself off to new ideas.

3. Try the plan for at least 21 days.

And, once you begin, be sure to:

4. Write your script out; practice before calls.

Pretty simple, right? Now we're ready to get to work.

❑ ❑ ❑ ❑

In order for you to become a successful salesperson, you have to prospect successfully. That's where the cold call comes in. Cold calling is the best and most economical way for you to develop leads on an ongoing basis. This book is devoted to helping you get in front of your prospects in the most efficient, profitable way. To do that, you may have to change some habits.

I'd like to take you with me to a typical sales office.

I visit hundreds of offices each year as both a salesperson and a sales trainer. I usually arrive early in order to get the feel of the office. If I'm doing a training program, I might arrive two hours before the program is scheduled to begin. This gives me ample time to observe the salespeople. I find that the most experienced ones are really creatures of routine.

Sam, for example, has been selling for the last twenty-five years. He shows up, with his morning coffee in hand, around eight in the morning. He gives himself an hour to gossip with the secretary, read the paper, and do a crossword puzzle. At the stroke of nine, he begins calling.

Marty, on the other hand, tends to come in a little bit later, but stills shows up well before 8:30. He uses his half hour to mail out literature to clients he's spoken to earlier.

Susan, who's brand new to the selling field, usually arrives right around 8:55, just in time to pick up the phone and begin her day.

Then there's Peter, who's been selling for a number of years, is very successful, and traditionally hits the office around 9:25, gulps down a cup of black coffee under the eye of his time-conscious sales manager, and plunges into his phone calls.

You may ask yourself what all these people have in common. The answer is—habit. More specifically, day in and day out, they each begin their morning in a certain way. This may seem harmless enough. You probably do the same thing. However, if your routine resembles those of Sam, Marty, Susan, or Peter, I'm going to suggest that you alter it. Why? Let me answer that question by posing another one.

Do you like sports? Any kind of sports at all?

Well, if you play tennis, basketball, baseball, or jog, or even walk briskly now and then for exercise, you know what those first few minutes on the playing court are like if you have not warmed up.

If you show up early for a baseball game, you know that the players are there a good two hours before the game and are warming up on the field.

They've all been playing for most of their lives. They're all experts at the game.

So why do they warm up?

If you know any musicians, you're probably aware that even a top concert pianist practices for hours and hours each day in order to stay successful.

My point is that as a professional salesperson *you should be warming up* before beginning your calls.

Let's go back to Sam, who comes into the office at eight. Most offices have a Sam. Because he's been making cold calls for over twenty years, Sam knows exactly how to best go about it. For him. There's no denying he's a pro. But even with all that experience, he's not taking into account something he knows very well.

If you start in abruptly without any preparation at all, then those first few calls you make are, like it or not, your warm-up calls. They're simply not as effective as the calls you make once you get into the swing of things. So, if you're going to make them *anyway*, why choose to make them to potential prospects who deserve your best shot?

Sam, of course, will have none of this. And very often, Sam will, twenty-five years or no twenty-five years, strike out spectacularly on his first few calls of the morning. This is that kind of morning. Five secretaries he's called on have hung up on him. What does he do? Sam stops his scheduled calls and calls softer customers who'll at least give him a friendly reaction. Maybe not an appointment, but a friendly reaction. If you ask Sam what's going on, he'll say, "Why should I get rejected first thing in the morning?"

It's a good question.

Let's take a look at the other people.

Marty, who comes in around 8:30, won't pick up the phone until after nine. Nobody in this office, it seems, will. If you ask Marty why this is, here's what you'll get: "Businesses aren't open until nine. You can't reach anyone."

That's bull. It may sound good, but it's still bull. (As we'll see, calls placed before nine in the morning have a *greater* likelihood of reaching decision-makers, because many of the most ambitious businesspeople come to work before their secretaries do.)

At 9:01, Marty starts to dial. He, too, has done absolutely nothing to warm up for the call, and he's not prepared for anything that's going to take place. But if we ask Marty if he might be better off loosening up a bit before starting his calls, he'll say, "Oh no; I've been making these calls for so long now that I warm up just by dialing the first three or four prospects."

By now my point is clear. Those three or four calls are worth money to Marty, money he's basically decided to toss out the window so he can get into the groove with the rest of his calls. My warm-up method is free; Marty's costs you customers.

Let's return to our sports parallel. Isn't the approach that Marty and Sam are taking kind of like going up to bat and letting the pitcher toss a fat pitch over the heart of the plate—and deciding not to swing? Batters like that are probably better off not even showing up for the game.

Let's go to Susan now. She's the one who rushes in at five minutes to nine, sits down at her desk, straightens it up, arranges her materials, and begins calling promptly at a minute past the hour.

Right around 9:03, however, she remembers some things she had to do, and stops making calls. By the time she gets back to business, she's so flustered, and so very busy, that she finds it nearly impossible to focus on her real mission: getting appointments.

Obviously, Susan could use a few extra minutes in the morning: not only for warming up, but also for planning her work day. It would be time well spent.

Then there's our friend Pete, coming in late as he does every day. He's slow and methodical about what he's going to do on the phone today, and he's successful, no doubt about that. But he's thrown away right around seven percent of his possible sales time by missing that first half hour. Seven percent a day, times five days a week, times four weeks a month, times twelve months—you get the idea. It adds up. And when he *does* begin calling, he'll be no better prepared than his co-workers, because he won't have practiced either.

Suppose I told you that before you started your sales day, you had to stand up and sing a company song. How would you react?

Whenever I ask that at seminars, people laugh. The fact is, though, in 1950, the IBM sales force began a policy of standing each morning to sing the IBM sales song in order to motivate themselves. There's an idea the Japanese stole from *us*.

Recently, at a seminar I was conducting, a manager of a retail operation asked me how he could more effectively motivate his staff. I suggested that every morning, before opening the doors of the store, he line all his people up in front of the sales counters.

"Walk around the store and point out new merchandise," I told him. "Explain the new promotions the store is offering that day. Inspect your salespeople for cleanliness and appearance. Turn the music up loud over the PA system so there's some excitement in the air when they first walk in. Generate some enthusiasm!"

He said it sounded like a good idea, but didn't think it would work for his store. I made a $100 bet with him. On one condition. He had to try this for twenty-one days. What do you think happened?

At the end of the twenty-one days, he had a more motivated staff. They were enthusiastic every single day. And most important, they were selling more. They were able to leave their cares at home and focus their attentions on the job first thing every morning. In short, they became more productive.

They were ready for the first sale of the day because they had actually *worked* in that twenty or thirty minutes before the door opened. Another interesting thing happened: when the manager decided he was going to discontinue the morning ritual (after all, the bet was over)—the salespeople became *incensed*.

They wanted to know why he was stopping something that had been so successful. They actually looked forward to the morning warm-up, and they looked forward to coming in to work each day because of it. It had become—are you ready?—*fun*.

❏ ❏ ❏ ❏

Most salespeople don't warm up at all. Salespeople, traditionally, are loners. They tend to come into the office and sit in the corner, dialing away, making calls and keeping to themselves.

If you've ever been in a telephone "boiler room," where there are hundreds of operators making calls, you know that the team spirit—of both competitiveness and cooperation—helps motivate each individual to make more sales.

You can do the same thing on your own. You can begin to develop ways in which you can motivate yourself more successfully during your first fifteen minutes at work, because *that period sets the tone for the rest of the day.*

But why should you?

The most important reason is that you're going to make more money in your sales efforts. But there's another, underlying reason that has to do with attitude—and habit.

If you have a lawn, you know that weeds have a way of popping up. It's frustrating. But weeds seem to grow, even in a lawn where nothing else will.

In fact, if you don't water the land, if you don't cultivate, if you do absolutely nothing at all—weeds will prosper.

It's almost as if they *know* that they can grow without you.

If you want to get and keep a lush, green lawn that looks naturally beautiful and feels wonderful when you lie down on it, you have to work at it. Constantly.

The grass needs cultivation. The grass needs you. It needs you to pull out the weeds, and sod it, and fertilize it. Unless you do, that effortless-looking, uniform beauty will run into dandelions. The lawn needs cultivation just to keep looking beautiful. How's that for contrast?

The lawn that looks great always needs work. The lawn that looks terrible never needs work.

What does it tell us about our selling effort? Unless we continue to work each day to improve our ability, the bad habits are going to creep in, by themselves, *without our help*. And we know that we don't need any more bad habits.

Remember: the telephone is an important instrument that you can use *every single day* to your profit—if you use it successfully and consistently. Later on in the book, I'm going to give you some actual scripts that will be effective in helping you to do just this.

❏ ❏ ❏ ❏

To be successful at the telephone every morning you come to work, come early.

Get to the office by 8:15 a.m. That probably means you're going to have to get up a little bit earlier, so let's begin with how you get up.

If you listen to the news upon awakening, you're probably making a mistake. The first hour of the day is the most productive hour that your mind has, since it is free of other thoughts. You can program yourself to have a more effective day by using that hour wisely. If you listen to the news on the radio, or to some meaningless music, you're not helping yourself become more enthused or productive.

Instead, go out and buy some sales-related tapes and listen to them in the morning upon rising. Start your day with some calisthenics. (It doesn't have to be fancy. You don't have to run 22 miles a day in order to feel good about yourself.) Listen to the tapes as you exercise. Then you might select an appropriate, upbeat book to read. Don't read the newspaper. Believe me, if a new world war has gotten a head start on you, you'll find out soon enough.

Begin each day with a good breakfast. You don't have to eat a lot of food. Eat good food.

Don't start out with an empty stomach and grab something to eat at the office. *The office is a place for you to work, not a place for you to eat.* You may be asking, "What if I want to work through my lunch hour?" Here's my answer: don't.

How many times have you seen secretaries and salespeople sitting at their desk eating lunch? Ask why they're not out in the sunshine, reading, or just taking a much-needed break, and the response is, "I don't have time." Well, you *do*, if you know how to manage your time more effectively. Start the day on a good note, get to the office with plenty of time to spare. You'll find time to breathe again. Don't be a sloppy Susan who hits the office five minutes before she's expected to perform and wonders at the end of the day why she's behind in her calls.

It's an important point. As a salesperson, you may not punch a normal clock, but you do punch a mental clock. There is a time at which you plan to show up at the office. It's all right with me (and maybe even with your sales manager) if you can sell consistently while coming in fifteen minutes late every day.

But is it really all right with *you*? Being fifteen minutes late means you are losing fifteen minutes on your competition. (Sound tough? It should. We'll talk later about the ways that selling is like war, and we'll also discuss ways that you can train yourself and plan strategies against your competition.)

To be successful, you have to have motivation, strategy, and willpower. Hopefully, the dollars are effective enough motivation. The plan you develop is your strategy. And by developing a strong inner sense of success, from the moment you walk in the office, you'll strengthen your willpower.

Work a full day. Schedule that day accordingly. Understand that there are times during the day that you need for yourself. Don't be foolish and try to plan a twenty-hour day into eight hours. Strictly speaking, you know that you are not even going to work eight full hours. Give yourself ample time for lunch. Allow space in your schedule for problems to arise; nothing is more frustrating than getting stuck in traffic on the way to an important appointment.

Don't let the little things get you down and prevent you from succeeding. Worrying is something we all do, but if you're like everyone else, forty percent of your "worry time" is spent worrying about things that never happen. Thirty percent is spent worrying about things that can't be changed by all the worrying in the world. Twelve percent is over misinterpreting the feelings or words of others, ten percent is over your health, and only *eight percent* of your worry is over legitimate concerns.

Start to discriminate about worrying. It will affect your selling—and will affect you on the phone. Why? Because your emotions are conveyed over the telephone.

In a recent study my organization conducted, we found that the salesperson's attitude was conveyed over the telephone *twenty to thirty times more* than meeting in person. In other words, when we see someone in person and sound a little ill-at-ease, we can compensate for that with other elements of our appearance (for example, dress, grooming, or movement). When we speak to someone on the *phone* and we sound ill-at-ease, from the prospect's point of view *we are*.

Your voice is *all* the listener has to go on. So it stands to reason that if you feel down-trodden, you will sound down-trodden, and no one wants to talk to someone who sounds that way.

❏   ❏   ❏   ❏

Before you step in the office, check yourself in the mirror. If you feel sloppy or dirty, you'll come across accordingly. Make sure you look good; pretend you're going out on a sales appointment. You'll be surprised at how much sharper you feel.

Clear your desk of all miscellaneous items. If you don't need those papers, throw them away. Many salespeople with messy desks insist that such a work station represents an organized mind. That's bull. It doesn't work that way. If your desk is clear, you're more apt to concentrate. You need a pad of paper and a pencil within easy reach at all times to write down appropriate notes. Of course, your cold calling script (which we'll be developing later) should be clearly visible so that you can refer to it at a glance.

❏   ❏   ❏   ❏

Place a small mirror on your desk. Put it right in front of you and smile when you begin making your calls. This is *extremely* important: as we've seen, the way you sound determines whether or not your prospect will talk to you.

Warm up! On your own or with a partner, practice your script out loud for a few minutes. Make sure you're at the top of your form when you do get down to business.

Once you begin your calls, *visualize* yourself succeeding. Nothing can help you more than you seeing yourself as a success on the phone.

Listen. It may seem obvious, but listening is a skill many salespeople never develop properly. Here are some tips you can use to make sure that you are listening properly:

Limit your own talking.

Think like the customer.

Ask questions to clarify, not to confront.

Don't interrupt.

Concentrate on what's being said.

Take notes.

Listen for ideas, not words.

Don't jump to conclusions.

Listen for overtones and clues.

Smile.

❏   ❏   ❏   ❏

When telephone marketing and appointment making began in the early '50s, the telephone was still seen as an intrusion. Now the telephone is a way of life; businesspeople have come to expect being called during their work day. With the right technique, a list of leads, and a dialing finger, you can track down potential sales more profitably than ever before.

If you use your time more effectively, of course, you'll be able to do more of what telephone salespeople do best. The fact that you've purchased this book indicates that you have an idea of what phone sales efforts can do for a business, but for the sake of a common frame of reference, here are a few of the main points:

Successful cold calling can:

> Develop new business.

> Save money when compared to time lost on the road.

> Yield better results than door-to-door.

> Build contact networks.

Knowing what is possible, and having seen what bad phone habits can do to stand in the way, are you beginning to think of things that you do during your own sales day that you might change? Are you a Susan, a Sam, a perpetually-late Peter, or a Marty? Turn those images around—and you'll become more successful.

Of course, a change in attitude is only part of the larger picture of making the right moves as a salesperson. In the next chapter, we'll examine some specific, time-proven methods for doing what you bought this book to learn about: getting appointments.

CHAPTER TWO

Getting an Appointment

I'm sure that it would make you, as a salesperson, feel a lot better if I devoted a full chapter to listening, communication, and non-verbal skills. Many sales training programs offer such niceties when they begin their actual in-depth program of selling. But to me, the single most important goal of this book is to *help you get an appointment*. Because unless you can get the appointment, anything else I could tell you about selling would be wasted.

Every sales book on the market talks about all the great things that you should do when you're face to face with a prospect. But how do you get there? Until you get in to see him in the first place, what you do, how you look, how you shake hands, and anything else is irrelevant.

❑ ❑ ❑ ❑

In talking to successful salespeople about their work, I find that their success can be attributed to four factors. The first is prospecting skills; second is presentation skills; third is product knowledge; and fourth is personal and professional development. Getting an appointment obviously comes under the first heading; but for the sake of thoroughness, let's look briefly at the last three as well, in ascending order of importance.

Personal and Professional Development

Personal and professional development usually takes the form of lessons from tapes, books, and records, as well as other projects you take on to improve yourself and your sales performance. Obviously, these are necessary things, and the instinct to improve yourself should never be minimized. I pointed out in the last chapter that negative thoughts can enter a salesperson's mind quite easily, but it takes work to prevent those thoughts from taking root and becoming habits. This is where seminars, recordings and the like come into play.

Abraham Maslow, a famous psychologist, developed a theory about self-image that is worth mentioning here. Maslow's theory states that at the foundation of the personal hierarchical arc are maintenance needs. In other words, ongoing self-improvement is an inherent characteristic of a person with a good self-image. If you are not secure in the area of personal growth, you will probably not be able to sell—since selling requires both confidence and the maturity to retain one's poise in difficult situations. What the theory really means is that to be comfortable enough with yourself to enjoy sales as a profession, you must commit to steady work. You cannot "fake it" on this score for any meaningful period of time.

Every day, then, you should do something to improve yourself and your sales. When you're driving to an appointment, instead of listening to a baseball game or whatever else happens to be on the radio, why not listen to those sales-oriented tapes we spoke of in the previous chapter? (I've met successful salespeople who literally do not know whether or not their car radio works. They're too busy listening to the tapes to check.) This is one way to "psych yourself up" on your way to an appointment. And why stop there? Remember, the first few hours of the day are the most influential. If you listen to a personal stereo on the way to work, why not play your tapes then as well? You can use your time better by preparing yourself for the day ahead—whether it's in a car, on a bus, in a train, or even on a plane.

Product Knowledge

This is a topic of great interest to salespeople. After all, how can you sell something you can't describe? However, there are dangers in over-emphasizing product knowledge as an area of study for today's sales professionals.

I train a great many people, and the single most difficult group is technical people, such as engineers or computer experts. The fact is, they speak a language I don't really understand. The other day I was talking with a group of engineers, and to be quite frank, I had absolutely no idea what they were talking about. The point here is not that I should enroll immediately in an engineering course. The point is that, from the perspective of the potential customer, engineers and experts (and, unfortunately, many salespeople) often seem to be using code words that may function very well with other technical types, but do not convey much in the way of usable information to the lay person.

As a salesperson, of course, you must have a certain degree of product knowledge, but don't overdo it. Ultimately, the fact that you have tremendous expertise in the details of your product may not be as relevant as the fact that you can set up an appointment and discuss intelligently with your prospect the benefits of the item you're trying to sell him. Those engineers can sit down and try to explain "torque" and a host of other technical terms to someone like me, but if *you* try the same thing with a prospect, you'll find out quickly that most don't have the patience for an introductory lecture.

Here's an example of what I mean. If I said to you, "Lower left seven sensitive to percussion and heat," would you know what I meant? My bet is that you wouldn't—unless you happen to be a dentist, in which case you know that I need root canal work. When you use code words, you lose part of your prospect's attention. Some of the most successful salespeople I know are people who do not know their product as well as others might, but are extremely effective in getting appointments. A case in point is a stockbroker I know who does not understand the technical aspects of the market, but nevertheless knows how to get in the door and make an effective sale. He brings with him a partner who does have the necessary technical information.

All I'm saying is this: attention to the area of product knowledge is overrated in today's sales force. You, as a professional salesperson, are effective when you bring together the expert and the prospect. Your role is that of a conduit.

Presentation Skills

I would be foolish if I told you that making a good presentation to your prospect is not important. But in the overall scheme of things, it is still not as important as getting in the door—prospecting.

Still, presentation skill does account for an important part of the overall success that you are going to have. Many people practice their presentation constantly, using roleplaying, memorization and even videotaping to hone their "moment" with the prospect. I wonder if they realize that the ratio of calls to appointments is usually three-to-one—and sometimes even higher? If, for every three calls you make, you only get one presentation, where should your efforts be?

Prospecting

Without a doubt, the most important thing that you as a salesperson can do is to learn how to prospect effectively. (At the end of this section, I'm going to give you some numbers that will back up my enthusiasm.)

Prospecting is a numbers game which is constant in a salesperson's life. Once you understand how directly it affects your day-to-day sales activity, you'll never put off this important step again. Now, I understand the tendency to skip over this element of your job. In fact, I can list 101 reasons not to prospect, and I can only come up with one reason why you should. But it's a good one: to get an appointment which translates into a sale. *If you do not have an appointment, you cannot make a sale.* It's as simple as that.

❑ ❑ ❑ ❑

How does all this fit together? In a series of discussions I had with top salespeople, I found that the relative importance of these four factors could be weighted on a scale of one to 100. The results? Prospecting, which won hands down, accounts for approximately forty-five percent of the time, energy, and talent of the successful salesperson. Presentation skills and the training to make an effective presentation account for twenty percent. Product knowledge, too, accounts for twenty percent—yet many salespeople spend virtually their entire careers learning about the product. Finally, personal and professional development, another activity often overrated, only accounts for fifteen percent.

In other words, you should be spending forty-five percent of your energies in the sales week prospecting; twenty percent developing presentation skills and meeting with prospects; and twenty percent continually learning about the product or service your company offers. The remaining fifteen percent of your work week should be spent in personal and professional development, to keep yourself lively and refreshed.

A good friend of mine works for a large insurance company. He was doing extremely well, taking in nearly $200,000 in commissions yearly. He had quite a practice, and his office consistently rated him the number one salesperson. One day, he called me and said, "I'm in trouble. I wasn't prospecting."

What had happened was that he was making the money—and spending the money. He was taking lots of vacations and sabotaging himself in the process. After a while, he'd stopped prospecting altogether; he was simply not in the office enough to maintain his contacts or develop new ones. Number one or no number one, he now had no new leads. Prospecting, even for the most experienced salesperson, *has* to be done on a continuous basis.

Unless you're a sales god, you can't simply pick up the phone and immediately have people throw money through the receiver at you. Finding out who your prospect is, what his needs are, and how to address them does not happen instantaneously. It's a process that takes time. How much time? Obviously, that can vary quite a bit from salesperson to salesperson and company to company. But let's say that today is June 1st, and that it will take you approximately six weeks from the time you begin the prospecting activity to close a sale. That means no matter what you do, you will not see a dollar until July 15th, or six weeks later. However, if you do not prospect until June 2nd, you will not see the first dollar until July 16th. If you do not prospect until June 3rd, 4th, or 5th, you do not see the money until July 17th, 18th, or 19th. In other words, there is a direct correlation between the prospecting you do *today* and the money you will see *tomorrow*. Many salespeople fail to appreciate this simple formula.

Too often, salespeople look at the dollars that they have earned today and think, "Well, I'm making money." They are; they're absolutely right. They've made money today, but they have not generated income for tomorrow, and tomorrow will come. In about six weeks, if they haven't prospected *today*, they are going to find themselves without a sale. You must prospect the same number of clients *every day*.

Let's say it takes you fifty calls to make a sale. If you do not make your fifty calls within this week, *no matter what else is going on in your office, no matter how important your appointments are*, six weeks from today, you will not make a sale. It's easy to grasp. But most salespeople try to find a more complicated way to sell. Instead of dealing with the real numbers, they make up all kinds of figures, estimates, and projections. That's all very well. But if they do not make the call today, they will not have the money tomorrow. (Not that I'm down-grading the importance of personal statistics—they're essential! We'll deal with them in depth a little later on.)

Right about now you've probably felt the fear of God within you and are very eager to begin your prospecting. Before we start talking about the elements of that process, however, let me share a secret with you. If you were to pick up the phone right this second and start dialing every listing in the white pages from A to Z, and if all you did was to yell into the receiver the words "WILL YOU HAVE AN APPOINT-MENT WITH ME AT TWO O'CLOCK ON TUESDAY," you would get an appointment. Eventually.

In fact, let's carry it a bit further. Suppose that right now, you went out to any major street corner in any major city in the country and stood there with your hand out, looking forlorn.

Would someone drop a coin into your palm after a while? Sure. And if you held a cup in your hand, your results would get a little better. Of course, if you then put a sign on your cup that said "Please Help Me," you'd make more money still. And if you changed your strategy again, and used the sign on the cup while ringing a bell, you'd do better than that. Finally, if you rang a bell, held a cup with a sign, and thought up something to say out loud to the most promising people who passed you, you'd continue your climb into the realm of high finance.

Selling is an asking game.

At this point in one of my seminars, one participant asked me, "Mr. Schiffman, do you mean to say that you've made, say, a $50,000 sale—merely by *asking?*" "Yes, I have." I replied. "And that's all it is; you have to ask. But you have to ask a lot." (We'll define "a lot" in due course.)

If you don't ask, you're not going to get any appointments, and you *definitely* won't make any sales.

❏   ❏   ❏   ❏

How do you begin to make the prospecting phone call? There are five steps. First, you're going to get attention. Second, you'll identify yourself. Third, you'll identify your company. Fourth, you'll use a key phrase that will elicit a response you want from the prospect (namely, "yes"). Finally, you'll close by setting the appointment.

In order to begin this process, the development of your cold calling script, you'll need a pad of paper and a pen. Before you recoil in terror at the word "script," let's discuss it.

If you're like me, when you first started to drive, you were frightened. I remember quite vividly. I got into the car, turned on the ignition, and shifted into gear. I pulled out carefully, checking the side mirrors, and then slowly, slowly drove down the street. I came to a stop sign, then thought to myself that I had to stop slowly so as not to jar the passengers. And lo and behold, a car hit me from behind because I was so busy trying to remember what I had to do that I failed to see what was happening around me.

Once you familiarize yourself with it, a canned script or presentation will allow you to be aware of all the things that are taking place in your cold call. There will be no need for you to stop and think about everything that's going to happen. In fact, the cold call will eventually become an automatic action for you, one you'll become more and more adept at performing.

How about another example? Think of the last great play or movie you saw. Now, the actors probably weren't making up all the good dialogue on the spot. There was a script someplace. But did the characters *sound* like they had scripts? Of course not. Good actors never do.

You, as a professional salesperson, have to learn to act. You have to develop a script that is going to sound good. This means that you must practice.

The script is the most effective way for you to get the appointment. Use it on a continuous basis, day in and day out, forever. I want you to underscore that word "forever" in the book, because it's persistence that you need to be a successful salesperson. Persistence may well be the most important word you will ever learn.

We're ready to develop our script. On a separate piece of paper, we want to write down one line that will get the prospect's attention (step one). That's easy: the prospect's name. So write down "Hello, Mr. Jones" on your pad.

(In order for this book to work for you and for you to benefit from my guarantee, you really will have to write this out. Do it in such a way that you çan read it back to yourself. Reading from the book won't help you.)

The second item in the script will identify you and your company. Write one line beneath "Hello, Mr. Jones," that does this (steps two and three). Read the whole thing aloud. It could sound like this:

> "Hello, Mr. Jones. This is Peter Smith from the XYZ Corporation here in New York City."

That's all you need. Don't get any more complicated than that. Don't ask how the prospect's doing, whether he's got any time, whether you can talk to him for a second, whether he's got a headache. Just say hello and make the statement. (Of course, Mr. Jones may not pick up the phone himself; this makes your job a little tougher, and brings us to the important matter of how to deal with secretaries during a cold call. Some approaches are outlined in Chapter Five.)

The next thing to think about is some of the benefits that your company can bring to Mr. Jones' business. Why are you calling in the first place? Are you announcing a new program, introducing a service, offering a product, asking the prospect to become involved in something?

All of these are important questions. Your third sentence should provide the answer. Below are a few examples.

> "Mr. Jones, I'm calling you today to introduce our new telemarketing service, which is guaranteed to increase the effectiveness of your operation."

> "Mr. Jones, I'm calling to introduce to you our new collections system, which can reduce your company's bad debt by up to sixty percent and improve your profitability by redeeming old accounts."

"The reason for my call, Mr. Jones, is to introduce you to our new real estate selling program, which can help you sell your house faster."

"I'm calling you today, Mr. Jones, to introduce you to our new car buying service, which can help you make more money on your car sale."

"I'd wanted to get in touch with you, Mr. Jones, to introduce our new personnel service, which can help you find the people you need in your office and save you money."

Now comes the difficult part. What question can you ask the prospect that will get a "yes" answer (step four)? Well, let's see. If you ask him:

"Are you interested in saving money?"

you'll probably get a "yes." Everyone likes to save money. This is something that you and your prospect have in common; you should take advantage of that. Make sure that it's clear that you both agree on the importance of saving money. And if you ask him:

"Would you like to find out how you can best motivate your sales staff?"

it's a pretty good bet he'll say "yes" there, as well. However, if you ask him:

"Are you ready to sell your house with us today?"

you'll probably get a "no."

So your next question should be one that asks Mr. Jones whether he's interested in saving money—or reducing his operating costs, or streamlining his operations, or handling his distribution more cost-effectively. Each of those is likely to elicit a "yes" response. Your script should now look something like this:

> "Hello, Mr. Jones, this is Peter Smith from the XYZ Corporation here in New York City. Mr. Jones, I'm calling you today to introduce you to our new training program, which can effectively increase the overall profitability of your company. Mr. Jones, are you interested in making more money?"

What do you think he'll say here? You wouldn't have asked the question unless you thought it would get you a "yes" from Mr. Jones. But suppose you hear instead:

> "No. I'm not interested in making any more money. I'm not interested in having a more motivated staff. I'm not even interested in talking to you."

What's your response? Easy:

> "Thank you very much. Have a good day. (Click.)"

That "click" was the sound of you hanging up the phone. Don't continue the discussion; you simply don't want to deal with this individual. You want to deal with people who have positive attitudes, who are willing to make a commitment to you that they're interested in having a better-run operation. Someone you'll have to fight every step of the way isn't worth your time. Even if you somehow manage to make this appointment, in the long run you almost certainly will not make the sale.

But most salespeople at this point ask Mr. Jones *why* he doesn't want to make any more money. Who cares? He doesn't. Why keep pushing? He's just taken the trouble to *tell* you that he's not particularly interested in making more money. Just pass. Your time is too valuable for you to take turns talking nonsense with someone.

At home, my kids have two gerbils that run around continuously in the miniature ferris wheel in their little cage. They're very busy gerbils. In fact, they're absolutely exhausted at the end of the day. But they go nowhere.

I have a name for the sales technique that asks questions like this:

> "Can I ask why you're not interest in seeing your business do better, Mr. Jones?"

I call it gerbil selling. Gerbil salespeople run around in circles all day but get nowhere. Many of them have incredibly dramatic conversations on the telephone, engaging in all kinds of debates—even winning some of those debates. But they don't close their sales. Don't be a gerbil salesperson.

Now, if Mr. Jones tells you that he *is* interested in making more money, your objective is to close by setting the appointment (step five). To do it, you're going to say:

> "That's great, Mr. Jones; let's get together so we can discuss this in a little more detail. How about Tuesday at three?"

That's it. Don't complicate things. Don't offer a variety of alternative times or ask whether morning or afternoon is a better time. If it turns out that Tuesday at three isn't a good time for Mr. Jones, let him tell you that, and respond with an alternate time (and make sure you have that time on the tip of your tongue).

This system gives you the controlling edge that you need in order to be successful. Suppose you do what a lot of salespeople do, and say:

> "Mr. Jones, I'll be in your neighborhood next Tuesday
> anyway, and I'd like to stop by."

What does that convey? There's plenty of room in your schedule. You're not a busy person. You've got a load of time on your hands. You'll just be in the neighborhood, hanging around. Believe me, you don't ever want to convey that. Offer a specific time that you have open and work from there.

Remember: this is the last step in the process. Assuming that everything goes your way, your job now is to set the appointment and hang up. Even if Mr. Jones tells you that Tuesday sounds fantastic and he's been looking for something like your service all his life, the most you should do now is confirm the address, the date, and the time, and hang up the phone. Don't go into anything else.

I've seen many salespeople ask loads of questions only to have appointments cancel. Why? They talk too much. Don't chatter once you get the appointment.

By now you're probably saying to yourself, "Gosh, this is the easiest thing that's ever come down the pike. All I have to do is make these calls, and I'm going to get appointments!"

That's not going to happen, of course. Objections will arise from Mr. Jones' end of the telephone line. But an objection is *only an opportunity to sell*. It is not a rejection. In the next chapter, we're going to talk about objections and how to handle them. As it turns out, there are turnarounds applicable to every single objection you can get.

By the way, I've given you the toughest script. There is an easier one; you'll find it in a later chapter. It's called the soft sell. But the one I've outlined here is the most effective script I've ever come across, and it can work for you.

Before you move on to the next chapter, I'd suggest that you take what you've written so far and practice it. See how it sounds. Work it through. Test it. You must get it down pat before you make your first call. (Again, don't make any calls using this script now; finish the book first. But do practice— and keep the basic outline fresh in your mind as we go through the next chapters.)

After you've reviewed your script, you'll be ready for the next order of business: objections. This is the area that gives you the best opportunity to use and develop your listening skills. Once you've done that (and followed the rest of the advice in the following chapter), I think you'll find that turning objections around is a lot easier than you may expect.

CHAPTER THREE

Handling Objections

Whether you've been selling for a day, a week, or a number of years, you know that whenever you make sales calls, there are objections. But objections, as I've pointed out already, are really your opportunity to sell. They give you a chance to focus on the major issues that concern your prospect, and turn them to your advantage in order to make the appointment and, later, the sale.

An objection has to be treated as a hurdle. Nothing less. Nothing more. You must know how you plan to turn around each objection you face.

In hundreds of seminars that I've conducted for salespeople, I've encountered six kinds of objections that come up again and again. We'll be discussing them here; if you've been selling for a while, many may be quite familiar. Look closely at these, and at the ways you can "jump" each of these hurdles.

At the outset, let's agree that our purpose in cold calling is to get an appointment. It is not to sell. If we fail to get the appointment, then we are not successful. You can argue that there are ways in which you can turn around an objection on the phone and make a sale. That may be true in telemarketing (a topic we'll cover later), but our concern in this section of the book is something very different. We want to find out how to take the objection, no matter what it is, and turn it into an appointment.

As I've pointed out already, there are six major kinds of objections. Here they are, in order of popularity:

1. The Stall

2. The Hard One

3. The Easy One

4. The Doubter's Maneuver

5. The Reassurance Request

6. The Hidden One

Let's look at each one individually.

The Stall

When you're faced with The Stall, the prospect will say that he or she is too busy to make a decision right now. This is perhaps the most common objection. It stands to reason, then, that the strategy you develop to counter The Stall is going to be a major factor in your success as a salesperson.

The Stall's variations include:

> "Gee, y'know, I'd love to talk with you about this, but things are really going crazy around here just now. Could you call back sometime?"

> "I have to have some time to think it over."

> "Listen, I've just been told that I've got an important
> distance call on another line. Why don't you just
> your number to my secretary?"

The Hard One

The second most common objection is The Hard One. This is
when the prospect has more information than you do, and
uses that information to put a roadblock in your way. This objection is the one that will require the most work on your part;
to beat it, you need to know your stuff.

Some examples:

> "I already have a broker. I'm doing just fine with him."

> "We had a meeting with the CEO and decided not to con-
> tinue in that area."

> "Well, I would be the one to handle that, yes, but I'm
> holding all decisions on it until I work out a written
> policy."

The Easy One

The Easy One occurs when the prospect makes a conscious
choice to cut the conversation off quickly, but reveals a need for
your product or service. If you get stopped by The Easy One
regularly—in other words, if you hang up *knowing* you've un-
covered a need for your product but are unable to convert that
need into an appointment—you've got a problem.

The Easy One sounds like this:

> "I really don't want to get into this with you. Anyway,
> we'd need a three-day turnaround."

"I thought about that a couple of months ago, but I've been so busy, I just haven't been able to sit down and work a budget out. Sorry."

"The guys next door have been doing that for us, and I really don't think you could beat their prices."

The Doubter's Maneuver

The Doubter's Maneuver arises when your prospect won't (or can't) decide the questions you put to them—and is unwilling to suggest someone else who can. It's a toughie, because a variety of factors can lie beneath this objection, from low self-esteem on the part of your prospect, to bad organization within the company. (What if you're dealing with a small business that really *has* no "purchasing agent" or "office manager"?) And let's face it, overstepping one's authority is not a key to success in business. If you're speaking with somone who traditionally has *never* made a decision, it will be very difficult to convince him to adopt an aggressive approach to his business problems.

Here are some classics:

"I'm really not sure whether I'd make that decision, to tell you the truth."

"Actually, there are other people involved in this, but I'd rather you didn't call them."

"It's really not my area, but I'm sure they're not interested."

The Reassurance Request

The fifth objection is known as The Reassurance Request. Here, the prospect asks for a sign of credibility from your side.

It's still an objection, but it requires that you listen carefully to what the prospect is really saying, so that you can offer him the information he needs to proceed with confidence.

For example:

> "We can't do business until I see a written estimate."

> "The last people we dealt with were real jerks. We haven't done anything in that area since we cancelled their service."

> "It's just not in our budget, I'm sorry. But listen, out of curiosity, who else have you done this for?"

The Hidden One

The most difficult objection of all is The Hidden One. Why? Because it's a camouflaged version of the real objection, and can lead you down numerous blind alleys. It takes place when the individual on the line gives you a reason not to schedule the appointment—but isn't telling the truth. This one takes real work (and a little intuition) to overcome, because you must somehow size up a situation that your contact does not want you to know about.

Here are some specimens of The Hidden One, with what the contact *doesn't* want you to know set in parentheses.

> "Yeah, I'd love to talk to you about it sometime, but I really don't have time right now." ("I'm not the decision-maker, but would rather not put my boss on the phone now because I'm just about to step into a meeting with her.")

> "It's been a tough year. We're not budgeted for that." ("We're doing great. We're budgeted for anything we want. But I'm screening the boss's calls.")

"Mr. Jones would handle that, yes, but he's on vacation."
("Unbeknownst to you, I am Mr. Jones. I just had a
fight with a coworker and don't want to think about
anything but getting into my car and going home.")

❑   ❑   ❑   ❑

When making telephone calls, you encounter these objections
often; but I bet that right now you handle them differently than
you would if you were making a face-to-face sales call. My
question is: why?

Suppose you had driven a hundred miles to see a prospect
who proceeded to throw The Stall at you. Would you, after
driving two hours to get there, simply turn on your heel and
walk out if you were told that there was no time to see you that
day? Of course not. You'd have to turn the objection around
somehow.

During the telephone call, you only have two or three
minutes, tops, to make the appointment. In that time, you
must be able to respond quickly to objections. The only way to
do that is to have a response ready for a given objection *ahead
of time*. And you must be persistent in your efforts, or you'll be
wasting almost as much time as you would if you drove
around all day from prospect to prospect, smiling as people
shut the door in your face time after time.

Here's an exercise I want you to try now. On the next page
of your notebook, list *your* six most common objections. What
things do your prospects say to you that stop you cold? Which
of the cateogries I've outlined describes each one best?

On the facing page, try to turn those objections around.
What could you say that would change your prospect's objective from getting you off the phone to getting more information about your product or service?

❑   ❑   ❑   ❑

What you probably discovered in doing this simple exercise is that most of the wording you're tempted to use in turning objections around is much too complicated for a two-and-a-half-minute telephone call. And if you're like most salespeople, you also found that you began *selling*, even though all you wanted to do was get the appointment and *then* make the sale.

As I say, this is not an uncommon reaction to objections. Once salespeople see that wall being placed in front of them, it's almost instinctive to begin doing what they do best: sell. They don't realize that their job is first to turn the objection around.

One way out of this trap is to remember the three "R's" of cold calling. They are:

- Repeat
- Reassure
- Resume

If you can remember to Repeat, Reassure, and Resume, you can turn virtually any objection around and get a positive response from your prospect. In other words, you can get the appointment.

Repeat the objection to the prospect to make sure that he or she really understands it.

Reassure the prospect about the point that's been raised.

Resume your pitch and set the appointment.

Sounds too simple, right? The fact is, it's *very* simple . . . if you follow a proven technique developed in hundreds and hundreds of telephone calls.

Why shouldn't you address your prospects' questions on the phone? You want to meet with these people. It's to their benefit for you to do so, or you'd have no motive for trying to sell the product or service. The question is, how do you convince them of the fact?

Let's say, for argument's sake, that the prospect's objection is something like this:

> "Gee, I'm sorry, but I'm already very happy with my current service."

Review mentally the six types of objections; you can determine that this might well be a hidden objection. (Maybe his brother-in-law has been selling him the same thing for the last 22 years and the prospect's not about to change. But you don't know that. You only know that he says he's happy with the present service.) Or, you might be dealing with a really tough objection—number two—perhaps he's got a sweetheart deal and he doesn't want to change. Then again, he might be stalling because he's going on vacation in an hour and a half and he doesn't want to talk to you now.

All these are possible avenues—now what must you do to turn those objections around?

At this point, other sales-oriented books will suggest that you ask questions. I suggest you don't.

You're not yet in a selling situation. You're setting up an appointment. To get bogged down in asking questions at this early stage is unproductive; why should the prospect answer at all? To be sure, it is necessary to have a good rapport with your prospect, but you should get to that in a face-to-face appointment—not a telephone call.

Remember those gerbil salespeople, and don't become one of them.

How do you turn around an objection? Let's look at it again. The prospect says he's very happy with his current service. Stop and think for a moment; have you ever heard that objection before? You probably wrote it down in your

notebook a moment ago. Were you ever
who told you that? If you've been selling
week or so, the answer is almost certair
body says he is absolutely, positively 1
service, there's usually one flaw in that ͟͟ͅ .
shot at turning the prospect around.

Could you, in all honesty, then, say something that takes
account of the fact that *you know* the objection isn't as iron-clad
as it sounds? Perhaps you could say something like:

> "Mr Jones, before they saw what we had to offer, some of
> our best customers used to tell me they loved their ser-
> vice—the same thing you're telling me right now."

Well, if you can say that, why don't you? And while you're at
it, why not continue by saying:

> "And you know, Mr. Jones, when I get a chance to sit
> down and discuss this with you, I'll be able to show
> you ways in which we can effectively increase your
> productivity. Can we get together Tuesday at three
> o'clock?"

So what do we have? A turnaround which accomplishes the
strategies I outlined above: Repeat, Reassure, and Resume.
You've just said that other people have had the same experience that Mr. Jones has had; you've restated the objection
and gone on to reassure your prospect. Most important,
you've communicated the fact that you've been effective in
helping people save money, even though they were happy
with their existing service. Then you resumed your effort to
schedule an appointment.

Let's try another objection. The prospect says to you:

> "I'm really quite busy right now."

heard that a hundred times, perhaps a thousand times.
g the technique outlined above, you might respond with:

> "Other people told me exactly the same thing until I had
> a chance to show them all the ways we could save
> time and money by increasing their productivity, Mr.
> Jones. Can we get together at three on Tuesday so I can
> do the same for you?"

Look what just happened. You've turned the objection around, reassured your prospect that other people have felt the same way, and you've moved in for the close, which is the appointment.

You can use this technique for virtually every single objection you've ever heard (or ever will hear) in your entire sales career. Of course, you might experiment with another phrase that follows the three crucial steps of Repeat, Reassure, and Resume, but be warned. The *most* effective tool I've yet come across for turning around objections is this simple, straightforward phrase:

> "Mr. Prospect, other clients told me exactly the same
> thing before I had a chance to . . ."

It works. I promise. Why tamper with success?

❑   ❑   ❑   ❑

Perhaps you're thinking, "What about the guy who says 'Send literature,' or 'I'm just not interested?'" As you probably already know, such responses come with the territory of sales. These are legitimate objections you must face every day. Let's deal with the first one: the request for literature.

This is probably most common from the person who is simply looking to brush you off. Leaving that aside for a moment, let me ask this: do you *want* to send out literature? I ask that question all the time in sales seminars. Inevitably, salespeople tell me that with all of the mail they send out, very few pieces actually result in a sale. For my own part, I don't believe in sending out material.

A good friend of mine sells very successfully for a large life insurance company. The first thing he asks a prospect is always, "Mr. Jones, did you get my letter?" If Mr. Jones says yes, my friend responds by saying, "Hey, that's great, let me tell you what it said." If Mr. Jones didn't get it, the response is "Well, I guess it's still in the mail; let me tell you what it said."

Here's the point: in twenty-five years, my friend has never mailed out one letter!

I'm not suggesting that you use this technique. What I am suggesting is that it doesn't really matter whether the letter gets mailed in the first place. Now, if you want to mail material, go ahead. It may make you feel better, but I'm pretty sure it won't make the prospect feel any better.

Nonetheless, you need to have an answer when you're asked to "send literature." My suggestion is to say the following:

> "We don't send out material, Mr. Jones; instead, I'd like
> to see you. How about Tuesday at three?"

You're shocked! I can hear you now, saying: "My gosh, I actually have to say that? I can't say that." You're wrong. You can. And if you do, you'll reduce the amount of material you send out by 99%—and you'll get more appointments.

Now you have two ways to turn around an objection. That's my entire system. Simple, isn't it?

At this point in my seminars, questions usually arise. "Whole system? But what about the person who says he's not interested? How do you turn that around?"

You *don't!*

It bears repeating. If the person you're talking to says that he's absolutely, positively not interested in talking to you about your program or your product, *there's nothing you can say* except:

> "Thank you very much; have a good day. (Click.)"

You remember that "click." That's you hanging up.

It amazes me to see how many sales instructors teach that you must hang on to the phone until you hear your prospect's phone being placed (or, more likely, slammed) onto the receiver.

There is nothing so upsetting to a salesperson as taking part in a conversation like this:

> *You:* "XYZ Typewriters can save you quite a bit of money, Mr. Jones."
>
> *Mr. Jones:* "I told you, we already have an office copier! Don't you know how to listen, for God's sake?"
>
> *You:* "Well, actually, XYZ doesn't even handle copiers, sir . . ."
>
> *Mr. Jones:* (Slam.)

You get enough of that every day without asking for more.

You have to learn how to turn off the aggravation by *hanging up first.* Whenever someone tells you he's definitely not interested, say thank you and hang up the phone immediately. Don't wait. Never wait. Never wait for that dial tone; never wait to hear that slam; never wait to listen to that person who's nasty to you; never wait to be yelled at. It doesn't do you any good.

Perhaps you're thinking, "If I stay on the line, I might get a sale." Yes, you might. And you might grow horns. You might turn bright green. You might even have wings one day. But if you're waiting to sprout wings before you take a flight to San Diego for a vacation, you're going to have one long wait. Don't do it. Don't ask to be intimidated. When you know your prospect is not interested, it's over. Hang up. And once you remember that you're going to get nineteen "no's" for every "yes," it won't matter to you. More important, you won't get into long, irritating conversations that you're not going to win.

Let's put it on another footing. If you've been selling for a while, you're certainly no stranger to this issue. Well? Once you responded to a prospect telling you "No, we're definitely not interested," by asking, "Why not?"—what happened? Nothing. I'd bet that in every case, you wasted time and got neither an appointment nor a sale for your efforts. And if you did somehow get a sale out of it, I'd bet you remember that sale very well—*because it happens so rarely.*

In the long run, it's not worth the energy. Don't waste your time. Go on to the next call. Complete twenty calls every single day not matter what you do (we'll get into what constitutes a "completed" call a little later). That's a hundred calls a week. Numbers like that will do more to make you successful than wasting time by asking someone to yell at you. If you do, and end up completing, say, five or ten calls a day, it will take forever to make sales because you won't have the appointments. But you'll have some fascinating phone conversations.

❑ ❑ ❑ ❑

Here's a summation of the things we've gone over (plus a few extra hints) that you may want to copy in your notebook and keep for reference. In order to make effective appointments on the phone:

Never give out too much information.

Never try to turn around an objection by engaging in a full conversation.

Never try to sell on the phone.

Always plan your call by using a script.

Always listen for the most common objections.

Always turn the objection around: repeat, reassure, resume.

Always be positive.

Always be firm.

Always be one step ahead.

Always hang up first to avoid rejection.

Even if you follow all of these guidelines, the sad fact is that all salespeople—from the rookies to the seasoned veterans—do have some calls that look promising, but do not result in appointments. How do you minimize such problems? We'll find out in the next chapter.

CHAPTER FOUR

The Ledge

The techniques in this chapter provide some important insights on rescuing "lost" conversations. The Ledge system, which we'll be studying here, incorporates techniques developed over a period of years working with salespeople who got "shot down" during calls that seemed, initially, to be quite promising. You'll find that it can actually help you turn around some of the most costly cold-calling mistakes that all of us make from time to time.

We've already discussed the various objections we can get when we make a cold call. And we've also reviewed a highly effective tool that can help you turn around those objections. That tool, of course, consists of pointing out to the person you're trying to see that other people—people who eventually became customers—used to say exactly the same thing before they got the chance to sit down with you.

That response is, I can assure you, an extremely powerful weapon. Unfortunately, though, you can't simply use it once and expect the appointment to materialize. (Well, at least not every time!)

Let's say the conversation proceeds something like this:

You: Hi, Mr. Jones, Greg Carson calling from EDI Training.

Jones: What can I do for you, Greg?

You: Well, I'm calling to tell you about our training service, Mr. Jones, which can increase your company's sensitivity to customers, boost sales, and increase profits. One of our clients showed a 26% increase in 800-line orders after using our training for its operators. Does that kind of an increase sound like something you might be interested in?

Jones: Greg, let me stop you here. We really are not interested in that type of training, because we already train in-house.

You: You know, it's interesting you should say that, Mr. Jones. That is exactly what Faveral and Faveral, the hardware direct-marketing firm, said when I called them back in April. But they did take the time to see me, they did end up going with the training, and Mr. Jones, they did experience a dramatic increase in their phone orders.

Jones: You don't say . . .

So far, so good. But watch what happens next.

You: They sure did. And I'm just as confident our training program will work for your firm, sir.

Jones: Well, why don't you tell me a little bit about it?

You: Sure. At EDI, we offer various types of training; the one I had thought might work best for you would be . . .

An innocent invitation and an enthusiastic response—but this is the beginning of this cold call's downward spiral to rejection. That first objection may or may not be turned around for good at this stage. Whether it is or not, you should not go into your full-fledged sales presentation, as shown above!

Nevertheless, if you've been selling for any length of time, you know that the temptation to start selling right there, at that first "buy" signal, is overwhelming. But it is a temptation you should resist if your goal is to cold call successfully.

What happens when you jump ahead in this way? You give the client all sorts of information that may not be applicable at this stage. More important, you give him plenty of ammunition that will enable him to do what most business-people want to do when it comes to salespeople who call on the phone, and that is end the conversation.

Think about it: you'll almost certainly come upon one or more examples from your own experience. You talk along amiably, encouraged by the other party, who seems genuinely interested. You start behaving as though you were at an in-person sales appointment. You list all the advantages of going with you, answer every question—and then the person on the other end of the line backs off, and uses a fact you've provided to shoot down your presentation. It's all downhill from there. What started out as a promising exchange has become something quite different: namely, a salesperson digging himself deeper and deeper into a hole.

Obviously, the best way to avoid this problem is to stick to your guns in the first place and ask for the appointment, suggesting a specific date and time. But sales is not an exact science, and there are going to be instances where, despite your best efforts, you will find yourself digging that hole.

What do you do?

Well, to get out of any hole, the first step is to find a foothold, or a ledge—hence the name of this technique. For the purpose of illustration, let's continue our "flawed" conversation:

> *You:* They sure did. And I'm just as confident our training program will work for your firm, sir.
>
> *Jones:* Well, why don't you tell me a little bit about it?
>
> *You:* Sure. At EDI, we offer various types of training; the one I had thought might work best for you would be the one-on-one program. And . . .
>
> *Jones:* Oh; you know, I've wondered about person-to-person training. Still, that might be hard to get approved. We've usually stayed with video-based training.

The hole materializes! Now, you may be tempted to view this kind of response as a green light of sorts. After all, even if a minor problem has been exposed, the person is taking the time to discuss your service, and is even providing you with a little information. But suppose you respond the way many salespeople would:

> *You:* Well, that's something we can certainly discuss when we have the chance to meet in person, Mr. Jones. But the real point isn't the format of the training, but what it contains, and once you show your customer service people . . .
>
> *Jones:* Well, strictly speaking, they're not customer service people at all. You see, it's more of a sales force, more active. You know, I don't think . . .
>
> *You:* Oh, it works for salespeople as well. We work with a lot of salespeople, Mr. Jones.

Jones: No, really, Greg, I don't think we have a good match here. I'm sorry, I think I'm going to have to take a pass this time. But thanks for calling.

What happened? Here we had a contact who was asking questions—surely a good sign—and then everything disintegrated!

Understanding the cycle we've just described requires understanding the way businesspeople—successful ones, at any rate—think. They are skeptical, and it is entirely legitimate that they should be: someone who gets hoodwinked regularly is unlikely to become vice president of finance. What's more, they shy away from undertakings that do not seem likely to yield a tangible benefit, and they are zealous in guarding their time (their most precious commodity). If you allow your product or service to be perceived as something unproven and deserving of skepticism, something that seems unlikely to provide a tangible benefit, something that may only lead to time being wasted, your contact will probably back out.

Accordingly, you must, in most cold calling situations, decide not to get into long, detailed conversations that will only hurt your cause. If you find yourself in the midst of such a conversation, you must do three things:

1. Find the first negative—even a veiled and pleasantly delivered negative like "Well, we might have a problem there"—and overcome it as you would a standard objection;

2. Remind yourself that your goal is simply to initiate interest and get an appointment; and

3. Tactfully and professionally guide the conversation back in this direction.

You might think that there is a danger of losing the person's good will in carrying out that third step, but this is not the case.

As long as you are pleasant and show due respect for your contact, you will be surprised at how easily the conversation will return to the mechanics of when and how the two of you can get together.

It bears repeating that *entering the "sell mode" at this point is a serious mistake.* Overcome the temptation to turn your "great conversation" into an "automatic sale." During the prospecting stage—which is what we have agreed we are doing with our cold call, prospecting—rushing ahead to the later points will result only in your being rejected. You do not yet have enough information to make any recommendation at all to your prospect.

Here's how the conversation above might have turned out if the goal had remained, first and foremost, to set an appointment, and if the Ledge technique had been applied at the first sign of a veiled negative.

> *You:* Hi, Mr. Jones, Greg Carson calling from EDI Training.
>
> *Jones:* What can I do for you, Greg?
>
> *You:* Well, I'm calling to tell you about our training service, Mr. Jones, which can increase your company's sensitivity to customers, boost sales, and increase profits. One of our clients showed a 26% increase in 800-line orders after using our training for its operators. Does that kind of an increase sound like something you might be interested in?
>
> Jones: Greg, let me stop you here. We really are not interested in that type of training, because we already train in-house.
>
> *You:* You know, it's interesting you should say that, Mr. Jones. That is exactly what Faveral and Faveral, the hardware direct-marketing firm, said when I called

them back in April. But they did take the time to see me, they did end up going with the training, and Mr. Jones, they did experience a dramatic increase in their phone orders.

Jones: You don't say . . .

You: That's right. And I'm just as confident our training program will work for your firm, sir.

Jones: Well, why don't you tell me a little bit about it?

Mr. Jones has asked about the specifics of your training programs, but you don't want to get into that just yet. Instead, you will agree to his request, but talk in *persuasive but still generalized terms* about what your organization has done and can do.

You: Sure. EDI is the region's largest training firm; we've been in business since 1972, and our client list includes firms like Rubber Tubs International and Hygenic Foods. We've delivered very strong results with our programs at these companies, and all of our work is accompanied by a 30-day diagnostic program—added at no charge to you—just to monitor your staff's progress. We're doing some very exciting things just now, Mr. Jones, and that's why I wanted to get together with you. What would you think about trying to sit down and talk about this on Tuesday at 10 a.m.?

Jones: Now, is this one-on-one training?

Jones is pushing for specifics again, and you cannot dodge with generalities a second time. In this case, your best bet is to respond straight-out to the flatly posed question, and be ready for a negative.

You: Person-to-person training, yes, sir. That's what we've used to deliver sales increases of up to 26% in just thirty days.

Jones: Oh; you know, I've wondered about person-to-person training. Still, that might be hard to get approved. We've usually stayed with video-based training.

Here is where you use the Ledge.

You: You know something? That's exactly why we should get together. What you just said to me is exactly what the manager at Major Outdoor Equipment said. And the great thing is, after they sat down and heard what we had to say, they ended up going with the program, and they had some really dramatic results. Why don't I drop by this Tuesday—I can show you the letter I got from them.

Jones (after a pause): Hold on—let me check my calendar, Greg.

You can use this technique in any number of ways, adapting it to fit your own circumstances and needs. You might decide to pose a question in order to regain control of a conversation. ("Mr. Jones, can I ask you how many widgets you sold last year? Well, that's interesting—we were able to do 20% more than that with XYZ Company.")

However you use the technique, remember that it is designed to help you avoid the pitfall of having "great conversations" that never translate into appointments. If you keep your mind focused on your goal—getting in the door, not selling the product or service—and listen carefully for that first negative, the Ledge can work wonders for you. Some of our clients, in order to avoid forgetting the technique during a seductively long phone conversation, even go so far as to write the word "LEDGE" in huge letters on a three-by-five card and post it on the wall where they can see it during calls!

CHAPTER FIVE

Reaching Your Decision Maker

"This system is all very well," you may be thinking to yourself, "but none of the ideas you've talked about so far will do me any good if I can't get through to the person I want to talk to." And that's absolutely correct. In this chapter we'll look at a number of simple steps you can take that will maximize the amount of time you spend on the phone with legitimate contacts, and minimize your frustration in dealing with gatekeepers.

Let's acknowledge one fact right off the bat: decision makers are never going to be *easy* to get hold of 100% of the time. People in positions of authority are often active, result-oriented types who have better things to do than sit by the phone all day waiting for salespeople to call. What's more, many of them are going to make the assumption that, simply because you are a salesperson, you are an obstacle to their achieving important goals. We can use some inventive approaches to make our odds of getting the message through a little more attractive, but we can never expect the impediments to vanish entirely. They are there, and if we can't adjust to them, sales may not be the job for us.

That having been said, there are a number of "tricks of the trade" you can use to get through to the people who can grant you an appointment. If you use them wisely, you will increase your own effectiveness and, ultimately, raise your sales significantly.

Method One: Attack at dawn.

Here's the way it stands now. You start calling at 9:01. The contact's secretary settles into her desk at 9:01. You call; she brushes you off. What you may not have taken into account is that, often, *your contact has been in the office for an hour or more*, and has been fielding the few calls that come across the line.

I'm not suggesting that you start making calls at 7:30 (although I should point out that there are salespeople who swear by this). I am saying that if you start to call at, say, 8:45 instead of 9:01, you may be able to up your time spent talking with contacts.

Method Two: Leave a message and a time you'll call back.

If it's not overused, this can be quite effective. Instead of asking the secretary to have the contact call you, indicate that you'll call back at a specific time: "Well, I'm going to be hard to reach for the next day or two. Why don't I call back at 9:00 tomorrow morning?"

You might be told that the time you mention is a bad time, but often this will help you to schedule a better one. Again, as with proposing an in-person appointment, you have nothing to lose and everything to gain by taking the initiative.

Method Three: Call Mike Powers.

Use this method only if the secretary or receptionist is very difficult. Let's say you're looking for the Director of Human Resources at a certain company, but have no idea who it is. No one likes pressing a tough secretary or receptionist for information about who's who. What to do? One innovative approach is to ask for Mike Powers.

> *You:* Hi, can I speak with Mike Powers?
>
> *Secretary:* Who?
>
> *You:* Mike Powers—the Director of Human Resources.
>
> *Secretary:* No, no, there's no one by that name here. You mean Milt Cooper. He's Director of Human Resources.
>
> *You:* Oh, I'm sorry. Cooper. Let me change that here. Well, is Mr. Cooper in?

You may laugh, but I've been asking for Mike Powers for years now, and he rarely lets me down. I'm still waiting to be connected to an actual Mike Powers, let alone one holding the position I mention to the secretary. If it were ever to happen, the call could be treated like a standard cold call. (But write me if it happens to you!)

Method Four: Be nice to the secretary.

It may seem like an obvious step, but it is routinely ignored. Too many salespeople are convinced that their relationship with the secretary is going to be adversarial, and thus insure that it will be. Why save your pleasant, upbeat tone for the contact if you are going to be abrasive and confrontational with the secretary? Here is an instance where good phone manners and an empathetic approach ("Are things as crazy over there as they are here?") can really work in your favor.

Method Five: For the hard-core set.

This is an approach I advise you to use only when the other four have consistently failed, and you feel it is imperative to reach a particular decision-maker: it entails indicating, via a message left with the secretary, that your call concerns the company's competition in the marketplace.

How does this work? It might sound like this.

Secretary: ABC, can I help you?

You: May I speak with Mr. Jones, please?

Secretary: I'm sorry; he's busy. Who's calling?

You: Peter Smith of the XYZ Widget Corporation.

Secretary: And may I ask what this is regarding?

At this point, instead of mentioning your product or service, try saying:

You: I'm calling about DEF Group.

(You may not have to point out that DEF is the competition, but many secretaries may not recognize the firm you mention.)

Stop talking. If you're not transferred to your prospect at this point, the conversation might proceed in the following manner:

Secretary: Can you be more specific?

You: Just tell him that I'm calling about DEF; my number is 555-2684.

Again, stop talking. Don't give out any more information than you need to. Assume that she'll go into the office and tell her boss there's a Peter Smith of XYZ Widget on line one regarding DEF Group. You'll find that, time after time, that's exactly what happens. When he calls, of course, he'll learn that you have: a) done work with DEF Group; b) been referred to him by a friend at DEF; or c) learned of his desire to eclipse DEF, whichever is accurate and appropriate.

You'd expect this to backfire a lot more than it actually does. I called a large manufacturer of mailing machines after weeks of trying to arrange an appointment and asked to speak to the sales manager—my prospect. He wasn't in. The secretary asked me what my call was in reference to, and I mentioned the largest competitor the firm has. She said she'd be sure to have him call me. I knew she really had no idea what the call was about, but she did write down the name. Twenty minutes later my prospect called back to find out what my call concerned—and wasn't negative at all. He was genuinely curious about my call. Maybe he was confused. Maybe he thought I *was* the competition. But he called.

The point is, everyone wants to know about other players in their business field. And what you're doing, in both of these examples, is *using* the competition—in this case, the DEF Group—as a basis for your call.

Now, suppose the contact, on returning your call, gets upset with you and says something like, "Why did you make me call you? You told my secretary that this was the DEF Company calling. You misrepresented yourself."

In twelve years, I have received exactly one call along those lines from an irate prospect. Here's what I said:

"Wait a second. I happen to believe that I have a product here that you will benefit from. As a matter of fact, I'm positive of it. If you don't want to hear about it, I'll be glad to hang up.

But, Ms. Brown, I do recommend that you listen to what I have to say, because afterwards, I guarantee you're going to want to see me."

At which point I told her a little bit about the service my company was offering. And as sure as I'm writing this book, I did get an opportunity to sit down with her, and I sold her the service.

CHAPTER SIX

Soft Selling—Persistence and Enthusiasm

In this chapter, we're going to be discussing another way to make cold calls. Often, salespeople feel that the script I've outlined may be a little bit too rough. To address this, I offer a different approach here.

Suppose you had the opportunity to sit across the table from someone and describe exactly what your company does and why it does it well. The conversation might begin like this:

> "Hi, John. You know, I'm really excited by some of the things that we've been doing here at XYZ Corporation. Just the other day we came up with a new way to fix a widget. Actually, that same technique would work really well in your operation, too. Why don't we get together and discuss that?"

That sounds simple enough. Many times at sales seminars, salespeople ask me why they can't just call somebody up and explain that they have a great idea that they think the prospect should listen to. Why should getting appointments be like pulling teeth? After all, both the prospect and the salesperson are professionals. Nobody's trying to bulldoze anyone. The plain fact is that the salesperson believes the prospect could incorporate some profitable ideas into his operation by using the product or service in question. Wouldn't it be so much simpler to sell if we could only approach one another in that way?

Well, we can. There is nothing wrong with doing just what I've outlined above. And you know what else? Once your prospect realizes that you want to help him, there's nothing on earth to keep him from saying, "Yeah, that's a good idea; when did you say you could stop by?"

The soft sell can be a very effective way for you to introduce your product. But as you develop and use this technique, remember that even though you're going to sound comfortable and natural, you're still going to get to the point—which is to get the appointment. That's been the goal of every technique outlined in this book, and soft selling is no exception. There's nothing more demoralizing than having exciting, lively, funny conversations day in and day out, and then realizing that your schedule for the upcoming month is empty.

❑ ❑ ❑ ❑

Let's take a look at how the soft sell works. You pick up the phone and you dial the number for the ABC Auto Specialty Company. You ask for the proper person (or ask questions that allow you to get his or her name in the first place), and then you say something like this:

> "Hello, Mr. Jones. This is Peter Smith over here at XYZ Widget Corporation. Mr. Jones, recently we've been working with several companies, including the DEF Group, which I believe is also in your business. At any rate, we've had tremendous success in using our

widgets to increase their production. You know, I was
thinking the other day that this might be something of
interest to you, since we've had so much success
around the country with it. Do you think that I might
be able to stop by on Thursday at three so that we can
discuss it in more detail?"

Stop talking. Wait and see what the prospect says. The gamble
here is that the person's willing to strike up a conversation
with you. After all, you've mentioned his competition and you
seem familiar with his business. You've also mentioned something important about your product. What's he going to say?
Quite possibly something like this:

"Well, you know, I thought about that, but we don't really have a need for it." Or:

"Fascinating. The only problem, though, is that you've caught me at an awfully busy time. . ." Or:

"I'll tell you, that does interest me; why don't you send me some literature?"

Sound familiar? You bet.

Informal though they may be, these are the same objections
we looked at in the previous chapter. But don't be discouraged.
Merely continue with the same low-key approach:

"Well, Mr. Jones, you know, I've heard other clients tell
me exactly the same thing until I had the chance to
come out and show them what this product can do for
their bottom line. So what I was curious about was
whether we could get together on this. As I mentioned, I've got a slot open on Thursday at three; how
does that look for you?" Or:

"Well, we don't send out literature, but actually, I could
do even better than that. As I was saying, I have

Thursday at three open. Why don't I stop by then and
give you an idea of what we can do for you?"

Again, the key here is to stop talking and allow the prospect to
finish the thought you've put before him. More often than
you'd expect, the response here is:

"Hold on; let me get my book."

You've got an appointment.

❏   ❏   ❏   ❏

We mentioned a method in the last chapter for overcoming
resistance from a secretary by leaving a message regarding the
competition. The same idea can be adjusted for use in your
soft-sell contacts with potential customers.

By getting a person to admit that he is interested in the
competition—and everyone is—you can lock them into a conversation and get more appointments. I have to reiterate,
though, that you don't want to get locked into a conversation
that serves no purpose. Use your knowledge of the contact's
industry as a basis to win attention and highlight potential
benefits.

But suppose you don't really have that basis. Suppose
you've never even made calls in this market before. Then what
do you do?

Simple: use the market you know to get the prospect's interest.

"Hello, Mr. Jones. This is Peter Smith from the XYZ
Widget Corporation. Listen, I wanted to call and introduce you to our new widget—it's been used successfully around the country by other companies just like
yours. It's turned out to be a really strong performer
wherever we've tried it, and I'd like to stop by and tell

> you more about our successes with it this week. How's
> Thursday at three sound?"

What's happened? You've piqued his interest.

Here's the sequence. First, point out that other companies just like the prospect's or in the prospect's industry have used you successfully. Second, illustrate the history of success that comes with your product or service. Third, tell how the product or service can help the prospect's company. And fourth, ask for an appointment. I'm tempted to add a fifth step: don't get sidetracked.

Let's say you've gotten your first few sentences out and the prospect says:

> "Whoa; slow down. What is it that you do?"

No problem. You know what you do. Tell him.

> "We manufacture widgets, Mr. Jones; actually, we're the largest supplier of widgets in the United States today. We've had tremendous success with our widgets in companies just like yours. I was wondering, could I stop by on Tuesday at three to tell you how the product can improve your operation?"

You've conveyed credibility by answering his question, *and* you've asked for the appointment. (You *didn't* go into a long discourse about XYZ Widget's history, corporate culture, personnel department, or policy on sick leave for left-handed employees.)

❑ ❑ ❑ ❑

Don't be afraid to use a "rejection" to glean more information about your prospect. Again, the key is to keep in mind how keenly interested all businesspeople are in their competition.

When I worked at a brokerage house, I used to call up large corporations (say, the MNO Steel Corporation) and try to find out as much as I could about my prospect. I would call the person's office and say:

> "Hi, Mr. Jones, this is Steve Schiffman from the XYZ Brokerage House. Mr. Jones, I happen to have a report here on the PQR Steel Corporation, and I'd like very much to be able to send it to you."

Of course, the prospect would be eager to learn about what PQR was doing, and would ask that I send the report along. I would then ask:

> "By the way, Mr. Jones, is there any other information you'd like from us as long as I'm sending this out to you?"

And it so happened that Mr. Jones was interested in receiving stock information on 123 Oil, ABC Tires, and GHI Aerospace—leaving me with a pretty good idea of what companies he might currently be holding stock in. And even though I hadn't set up an appointment, I was ready for my next step. (Note that I was *not* sending him a brochure about the wonderful service he could get from my firm, XYZ Brokers!)

We might call the softer method we're examining here "talk-through"—you're not abandoning your script, merely talking through it. You're having a "gentleman-to-gentleman" conversation. I should warn you that this technique is used by a lot of high-ticket salespeople and is not really geared for the pressured selling environment that most of us face every day.

If you do decide that this method is for you, remember: it requires a much more relaxed approach. You have to slow down. You can't rush a soft sell.

At the same time, soft selling requires the same persistence in reaching the prospect as any other cold calling technique. Let's say you're stopped by something like this:

> "Gee, that's really interesting, but I'm afraid I'm not the person you want to talk to. You want Mary Brown, extension 123. But I should tell you right now, she's very tough to get in touch with."

Sounds simple enough. You say thank you, hang up, and call extension 123. Sure enough, Mary Brown is in a meeting. So you leave a message asking that she call you regarding the DEF Company (her competition).

Which she does. Two weeks later. After you've made hundreds of other calls and have no idea who Mary Brown is anymore.

Most salespeople can recall plenty of similar incidents. Many times it takes the form of a lengthy game of "telephone tag" ending in a confused and very loud:

> "WHAT? I'm talking to a SALESPERSON?" (Click.)

But let's return to Mary Brown. There you are, talking to someone whose name you remember dimly, if at all. You've got about ten seconds to answer a lot of questions. What status does this prospect have? How much have you said to them previously? What do you do to keep them on the line?

There are three ways for you to make sense out of this situation. One is to develop a special microcomputer and have it installed in your skull so that you remember every contact name and company you've ever dealt with. Not very likely. Another is to keep *great* records. I recommend it highly, but still, you don't have time to flip through nine different notebooks here. Finally, you can develop a standard set of responses—a "miniscript," if you like. One that gives you something to say and buys some time so you can figure out what the heck's going on.

When Mary Brown calls back, odds are that she really doesn't know what your call was in reference to. Nor do you know what she's been told. Although you've left your message, the secretary may have written it down improperly or passed it along through a third party. All she knows is that it has something to do with her competition. All you know is that some prospect, with whom you may or may not have spoken previously, is spending valuable time calling you back. It's probably not a good idea to ask her, first thing, if she wants to buy a widget.

I suggest you say this:

> "Ms. Brown; I was waiting for your call."

Tough, huh?

This phrase puts you in the driver's seat. What it says to Mary Brown is that you are important enough to justify her decision to return the call. Wait for a moment, then proceed with a pitch along these lines:

> "Ms. Brown, my name's Peter Smith, and the reason for my call is that I'm with the XYZ Widget Corporation here in New York City. We've been doing some work with other companies just like yours, and I wanted to suggest to you that I stop by on Tuesday at three to see you and explain some of the successes we've had. Would that be convenient for you?"

That's it. Stop. Let Mary Brown figure out why you called in the first place, and give her a chance to get a little upset. Certainly that's understandable in this situation.

A common response at this point it:

> "Well, I'm the wrong person for you to talk to. I don't handle that."

You counter with:

> "Oops; sorry about that. Who should I call?" Make sure you get the name and phone number of the proper person. If Mary Brown can't (or won't) connect you with the new prospect during your conversation, call back later.

Skeptical? Don't be. Follow the four rules. They're so important I'm going to list them again:

1. Finish the book before you do anything.

2. Don't close yourself off to new ideas.

3. Try the plan for at least 21 days.

4. Write your script out; practice before calls.

Salespeople usually have a certain amount of skepticism in their bones. They're jaded; they think they've been through it all before. You can't let that happen. You have to rejuvenate yourself each time you pick up the telephone. You have to rethink what you're doing. Every day.

Recently, my wife and I went to a Broadway play and were absolutely thrilled by the actors' performances. Afterwards, we wondered how the cast must feel—doing the same show every single night, month in and month out. We both agreed that it had to be quite difficult to do good work under those conditions.

But after some thought we came up with a couple of reasons for the actors' excitement. The first was that the audience was different every single night. Each new crowd was a fresh challenge. The second was that the actors had ob-viously developed the ability to look at their roles with new eyes before each performance; they'd learned to call on the same energy that comes with an opening night. Professionals know how to do this; amateurs burn out and eventually lose their enthusiasm.

Doesn't that sound just like a salesperson? Don't you know salespeople who burn out because of boredom? If they were actors, how long do you think they'd last on Broadway?

If you think about it, every morning, when you start your calls, you are performing to a new group of people. It isn't the same guy over and over again. It's someone who's never heard your pitch before, never even heard you *speak* before. You have to take advantage of a fresh opportunity to talk to that new person about something exciting. If you approach it that way, you *have* to be successful.

On the other hand, if you see yourself doing the same thing, day in and day out, to the same group of people, it *has* to be boring. Anything is boring under those circumstances.

Certainly you've known people who have boring jobs. The people who sell tokens for the subway, or who give out tickets to the kiddie rides at the state fair, or who park cars in crowded city lots twelve hours a day—they've got boring jobs. *You don't.* You're talking to new people with new problems and different businesses and unique personalities—every single day. If you treat those new people as exciting prospects for your business, success is the only avenue available to you.

CHAPTER SEVEN

Closing the Sale Over the Phone

So far, we've talked about setting up appointments on the telephone. In this chapter, we're going to take a moment to examine some of the techniques available to those salespeople who have to close their sales *over the phone*—that is, get the person on the other end of the line to say "yes" without any in-person meeting whatsoever.

To appreciate what goes into this kind of phone work, it's a good idea to break the whole process down into what I call the "phone closer's sales cycle." This cycle is a little different in application than the cycle that would apply to those who close their sales during an in-person meeting, but as you'll see, the basic principles will apply to just about anybody who sells something for a living.

It's possible for each of the steps I'll outline below to take place in a single conversation; accordingly, each step will explore a segment of one hypothetical call. Of course, your sales may require a number of calls before you reach the close, and not every call will encompass all four stages.

Let's take a look at the four stages of the cycle. Each stage is related to the whole process. The objective of the first stage is to get to the second; the objective of the second is to get to the third; and so forth.

Stage One: Qualifying

You and your customer determine that you're mutually interested in proceeding to the next step. That doesn't mean that you're certain the individual on the phone wants to buy your product or service—that only happens in Step Four, Closing. Here in the qualifying stage, we're simply making sure that the customer is willing to discuss the potential usefulness of the product or service, and we're also making sure that the individual or company in question is the type of account we hope to do business with.

In other words, we're overseeing the contact's transition from "suspect" (someone who may or may not be able to use the product or service) to "prospect" (someone whom we've determined could develop an interest in learning more about what we're selling).

What might this first step sound like in a conversation? I'll give you an example; the structure should be familiar by now. The individual approaches will vary, but the qualifying conversation (which takes place, of course, once we've gotten past the front desk, and perhaps even learned a little bit about the firm) could sound something like this:

Mr. Jones: Mr. Jones here.

> *You:* Hi, Mr. Jones, this is Peter Smith from the XYZ
> Widget Corporation. I'd like to ask you something
> about your widget service if I may.

> *Mr. Jones:* Let me stop you right there, Peter. I really have
> no interest in talking about our widget service.

> *You:* You know, Mr. Jones, a lot of people tell me that at
> first—before they get a chance to discuss with me
> some of the benefits we're offering. What I'd like to do
> if I could is ask just a couple of quick questions. Is that
> all right?

> *Mr. Jones:* Well . . . okay, go ahead.

The information resulting from such a conversation is very important—and marks our transition from the first to the second step. And, of course, once you find out that Mr. Jones does in fact have time to discuss widgets, he may fit your profile of a potential widget user, and the fact that he said he had no need to discuss the product at the beginning of the conversation carries less weight.

On the other hand, if the conversation I've outlined above concludes a little differently, say, like this:

> *You:* . . . What I'd like to do if I could is ask just a couple
> of quick questions. Is that all right?

> *Mr. Jones:* No. I don't care what you want to ask or how
> quick it is. Goodbye. (Hangs up.)

. . . then Mr. Jones is not a prospect. Once upon a time, he might have been able to be a prospect, but he sure isn't one now. He is, instead, a dead lead. He's no longer in the process. And that's okay. There have to be dead leads for there to be live ones. It's part of the cycle.

So what we're looking for at this stage is the determination that someone we've contacted by phone has agreed (perhaps implicitly) to go through the cycle and discuss the product with us.

Stage Two: Interviewing

This is where we find out the needs of the individual in order to determine what we'll say later on. Step Two is analagous to an in-person interview in the types of sales discussed elsewhere in this book, and it's probably a good idea to think about it in these terms while you're selling on the phone. Why? The data you're asking for is crucial, even though you may be asking for it in virtually the same breath with other, less important questions (like, "What number have I reached?"). The information you gather will allow you to pinpoint the specific product, program, or service that you're going to be offering your prospect.

Typically, there are three basic questions to ask at this stage. But before you start asking them, you must make a smooth transition, and give your prospect the chance to find out a little bit more about you.

> *Mr. Jones:* Well . . . okay, go ahead.

> *You:* Mr. Jones, let me tell you a little bit about us. We've been in business for the last six months (two years) (ten years) (two hundred years) (whatever), and we happen to be the best widget company in the world. And today I was just curious to find out a few specific things about your company's widget use.

> *Mr. Jones:* Shoot.

> *You:* Okay. *(Question Number One—The Past:)* Have you ever worked with XYZ Widget before?

Mr. Jones: Well, yes, once we did, back in 1979.

You: How did it work out?

Mr. Jones: Hmm . . . I can't recall any problems with it whatsoever, to tell you the truth. A couple of years after that, of course, we had some budget cutbacks; you know how it is . . . eventually we re-established our widget service, though.

You: Uh-huh. *(Question Number Two—The Present:)* What are you presently using?

Mr. Jones: Well, presently we use the old Skipperoo widget, which isn't really effective, now that I come to think of it . . .

You: No kidding. *(Question Number Three—The Future:)* Tell me something; does your discombobulating department forecast much additional use for widgets in their work over the next six months or so?

Mr. Jones: Funny you should ask about that. I was just talking to Roger Gardner over in Discombobulating this morning; he said that now that they've landed the new rediscombobulating project, they'll be taking up most of our available widget time, and we might have some logjams if we're not careful.

(And, given that information, Step Two might proceed along these lines:)

You: Is that right. You know, a lot of people working on the kind of project you've described typically find that we can help them with one of two types of widgets that I could tell you about. The first is our top of the line item, our model X-42.

Mr. Jones: How much is it?

You: That runs a little over three quarters of a million dollars.

Mr. Jones: Sounds kind of expensive . . . I don't think we'd be interested in that.

You: Oh, okay. Well, the second one, the X-43, which also delivers superior results, is a little bit less expensive; it only runs nine dollars and ninety nine cents. But it happens to have excellent pickup and great rediscombobulation; it might be just what you need.

Mr. Jones: Hmm . . . that might work.

In a number of your calls, the second stage will conclude with just such an affirmation on the part of the prospect, a "that sounds okay" kind of reaction. This allows us to move on to the next stage.

Stage Three: Presentation

This is where we supply more specific information about the benefits of the product or service, being careful not to assume that the sale has closed—because it hasn't.

Up to this point we know two things: the person we're speaking to is in fact a prospect, and he or she has agreed that the product or service might have an application. That's it. We now proceed in a clear, calm, non-threatening manner to the highlights of the product or service.

What, exactly, do you say? Of course, there are a lot of things you can offer the prospect at this point, but really, the only things that make any difference can be broken down into three main categories: *features, benefit,* and *proof.* A *feature* of the X-43 might be that it's easy to clean. A *benefit* would be that it lets the user increase production (and *not* that it has, say, a high input-output rate—that would be another *feature*). And *proof* of the X-43's usefulness might be the fact that it was singled out for an industry honor by a trade magazine.

All three concepts are important, but of most immediate interest to your prospect is *benefit*.

Many salespeople confuse the customer *benefit* with either of the other two areas. *Features* and *proof* are important, but what your prospect really wants to hear about is how the product or service you're offering will actually help him or her. So you should know exactly what your *benefit* is and be able to discuss it at the drop of a hat.

Let's examine how *benefit* differs from *features* and *proof*. Consider other products people buy—and why they buy them. Consider, say, green rubber boots.

Why do people buy green rubber boots? Well, now. *What* are they buying?

You could come up with a list of things *connected* with green rubber boots: the color, the lining, the strength of the seams, the thickness of the soles. But are these the actual *product*, in a fundamental sense? I say no. I say they're *features*. They're part of the *why*. They aren't the *what*.

There's another important element that enters into any discussion about the green rubber boots: the manufacturer's reputation. You know—the fact that the product has good "word-of-mouth," or that the company that makes the green rubber boots has been in business for forty years, regularly getting top marks in *Consumer Reports*.

But, again, that's only a contributing factor to the decision to buy green rubber boots. It's a very important part: the *proof*. But it's not what someone actually purchases. It's still part of the *why*.

Think of the *problem* solved by a pair of green rubber boots. You're stranded at rush hour in front of a shoe store. It's pouring out. You're wearing a pair of tennis shoes. You look in the window and see a beautiful pair of green rubber boots. You decide you can afford them. You walk in and buy a pair. *What have you really bought?*

Dry feet!

That's the *benefit* of green rubber boots. That's what the shoe store really has for sale.

What is the *result* your product or service offers? What saves a client money? Makes his or her business more productive? Creates more profit? Whatever it is, that's the *benefit*. The *benefit* is different from *how* the savings, productivity, or profit is delivered. *How* is interesting—and important—but it's not the *benefit*.

From the prospect's (read: customer's) point of view, the whole question of "to buy or not to buy" boils down to a simple three-way analysis—a triangle, if you will, with the *benefit* at the apex.

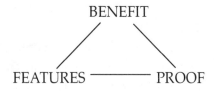

Benefit (you get home with dry feet). *Features* (thick soles). *Proof* (your sister-in-law swears by these rubber boots).

Try it now—fill in the blanks using your product or service.

After having specified, in no uncertain terms, the *benefit*, we can move on to the supporting concepts of *features* and *proof*. Here's how it might sound.

> *You:* Mr. Jones, let me tell you a little bit about the X-43 *(Benefit:)* It will help you increase production by as much as twenty percent. *(Features:)* That's because it requires less maintenance, it's easy to clean, and it has the highest input-output rate of any widget in its class. *(Proof, part one:)* It also happens to have been selected by *Widgets Monthly* as the top widget of 1991.

This alone may or may not be enough to sway the prospect; accordingly, we must be prepared to bolster our presentation with another dose of *proof.* (*People proof,* if you will.)

> *You:* Mr. Jones, let me give you an example of how other people like you have used the X-43. Sam Smith at Ellem Enoapy Corporation uses the X-43 exclusively, and has told me he will never buy another widget from anyone else as long as he's handling their purchasing. For my part, I think this product is something that could benefit your company, too.

Now, it would be nice if, at this point, Mr. Jones automatically recanted, apologized for his initial skepticism, and, having seen the error of his ways, asked us for details on when he could receive 5000 X-43's. Unfortunately, it doesn't always work that way. After our initial discussion of what the product has to offer, we can expect to confront an objection or two.

Most of us are so busy trying to present the product that we forget to handle the objections properly. You may want to review the appropriate sections of Chapter Three to determine which techniques will be most effective for you in your closing efforts. Of course, the primary principle—Repeat, Reassure, Resume—is just as valid in phone sales as it is in prospecting.

Let's look at some of the specific objections people who sell over the phone will face—and see how best to address them.

When your prospect tries to stall, the best approach is usually to offer a specific timetable for further action on the matter. (This will not only leave you with a clear view of your next step, but also help to smoke out those who are simply too wishy-washy to tell you they aren't seriously interested.) When the objection is that the product or service costs too much, you usually have three options. You can discuss the advantages of a lower-priced version (as we did above in recommending the X-43); you can pro-rate the cost over time to put it in the proper perspective (i.e., point out that the X-43 will end up costing only a few cents a day over the course of a year); or you can compare your price to that of a competitor or to the "cost" of continuing to do business without the product or service.

Of course, you may get an "objection" that's vague or unclear, leaving you with no idea of how to proceed. In these cases, it's generally best to come out and ask the client where the problem is. But *how* you ask is vitally important.

> *You:* Mr. Jones, is there anything I didn't explain clearly enough about the X-43?
>
> (. . . is there something I should know about your present widget service?)
>
> (. . . is there anything I might have left out about how the X-43 can help boost your production?)
>
> (. . . did I do something wrong?)

Don't ask the prospect whether or not he or she "understands" what you've said so far. (It places the prospect in an awkward position—who wants to admit not understanding something?) By using the techniques outlined above, we're likely to get a response like this:

> *Mr. Jones:* Oh, no, it's nothing on your end—the only thing is, I've got something of a problem with this because of . . .

. . . and then, of course, Mr. Jones will probably give you more information, allowing you to fine-tune your approach.

As we've already seen, some objections are tougher than others. It will be very difficult indeed to turn around an objection like this:

> *Mr. Jones:* You know what? I just picked up one of your competitor's products last week, the Blattworth Mach Nine Widget. I got it for nothing; my brother works for Blattworth.

On the other hand, many objections will be considerably easier to handle, especially if the prospect is reminded, wherever appropriate, how "other people said exactly the same thing."

> *Mr. Jones:* We like the color red here at our company, and all the widgets I've seen have been blue.
>
> *You:* Actually, that's no problem, Mr. Jones. A lot of our customers prefer red widgets—that's why we've come out with seventeen different shades of red on the X-43.

Whatever the objection, you must remember that objections are part of the sales cycle. There's no personal dig at you if Mr. Jones' brother works for the competition. It's one of the many, many objections you'll encounter over the course of a day. Some of them you'll be able to turn around; some you won't.

If we've done everything properly up to this point, we'll be able to think about proceeding into the final stage of the cycle.

Stage Four: Closing

For some reason, salespeople tend to hem and haw a great deal when it comes to closing. And that's unnecessary. If the proper groundwork has been laid, and if the prospect has determined that the benefits of the product or service are genuine and that the relevant objections have been met, closing the sale is quite simple. It could sound something like this:

> *You:* Mr. Jones, you know what I'd like to do? I'd like to get that paperwork started now so that we can be in business next week.

We make the assumption that the sale will close. We *ask* for the sale in terms the prospect will find unthreatening. We try to initiate paperwork. It's that simple.

Will we get shot down? Sometimes. But what's the alternative? Continuing to prattle on about how wonderful our widgets are? *The prospect has heard that already!* Ask for the sale. Then stop talking and see what kind of answer comes back.

Of course, some prospects won't immediately hang up on us at this point, but won't be ready to make out a purchase order, either. Their answer to the first "can-we-get-started" attempt will determine our next move in the close. Here are some approaches we might take:

> *The Downscale Model Response:* I can certainly understand your hesitation on the X-42, Mr. Jones; three quarters of a million dollars is a lot of money. But you know, a lot of our clients felt just the same way at first, before they learned about the X-43, which delivers superior performance at a very competitive price.

> *The Future Response:* Mr. Jones, one of the reasons I'd wanted to try to wrap this up is so we could lock in your rate; it seems like every month or so that the ac-

counting people raise the prices on us, and I felt sure you'd want to avoid that.

The Incentive Response: Mr. Jones, why don't we think about giving you a free service contract on your widgets for the first year? (Note: If your sales manager has a problem with maneuvers like these, you may have to come up with a more creative approach to this kind of close, such as dropping by the prospect's house and washing his car or her car every Saturday— or offering to put your first born child into servitude with the prospect's firm.)

The Endorsement Response: Mr. Jones, as I'd mentioned earlier, Sam Smith over at Ellem Enoapy Corporation is very happy with the X-43. Maybe we could set up a conference call that would give you the chance to talk with him about his perceptions of the product. What do you think?

In future chapters, we'll talk about personal sales statistics and cold calling. For phone sales work, too, there are standards you can try to meet, figures you can use to gauge your success. You might have to make 100 "completed calls" (a term we'll discuss in more detail later on) to reach 50 prospects. About 60% of those prospects will be qualified ones, and from that pool you can expect to close two sales.

Here are some other ideas that may help you close more effectively over the phone.

Develop a set script that will allow you to standardize your approach.

Take notes.

Listen to the prospect, don't interrupt, and try to think like a customer; remember to repeat an objection so that the prospect knows that you heard it and that you understand it.

Keep your tone conversational; nothing turns people off more quickly than the perception that they're speaking to a machine.

Don't apologize for making the call in the first place.

Prepare yourself for the common objections you'll face, and don't let them take you by surprise.

Finally, bear in mind that telephone sales work is focused on one thing—sales. Don't get sidetracked. Don't be seduced by "great conversations." Just go from one step to the next, and realize that all four are interrelated. If you're in the middle of Stage One, work toward preparing yourself and the prospect for Stage Two. Proceed in this way throughout the cycle. If you do, you'll be successful.

Chapter Eight

"How'm I Doing?"

The former mayor of New York City, Ed Koch, used to walk around the city asking his constituents, "How'm I doing?"

Why do you think he did that?

Let's be honest: he had a difficult job. And sometimes it's hard to tell how a politician is doing. Perhaps Mayor Koch was trying to get a continuous "read" on the level of his performance—so he could do his job a little bit better.

Let's say the tables were turned. Let's say that you were walking down the street and someone came up to you and asked, "How're you doing?" With regard to your performance as a salesperson, how would you answer that question?

Many sales trainers tell you that you must always be sunny and positive in such matters, under all circumstances. If you listen to them, your response is a simple one: "Everything is *great!*" But is that really the way you want to answer the question? What if it were possible to be a little more accurate?

Suppose you could say something like, "Well, I completed fourteen calls yesterday, got two appointments, and made one sale, amounting to five thousand dollars of income in my pocket." It would be a more useful way to rate yourself than just saying, "*TERRIFIC!*"

I think that the most neglected lesson of all in sales is the importance of keeping track of one's personal statistics. Many promising salespeople fail to comprehend that they are doing themselves a disservice by ignoring their own numbers. They look at statistics as something a sales manager keeps in order to "get" them.

In this chapter, we're going to focus on specific ways for you to predict your own success accurately. You'll also learn to monitor yourself on an ongoing basis so that you'll never need a sales manager's help again. Once we're done, you'll be able to forecast your own success on a quarterly basis.

First, let's define what we mean by success.

If you were to come into my office, you'd see a wide variety of plaques and trophies that I've received over the years. Everything from tiny plaques for a small presentation that I made, to large plaques for something that took many years for me to achieve. I even awarded *myself* a large American flag once for outstanding performance. (Remember what I said in an earlier chapter about self-renewal? Proper recognition is part of that.) All of these are fantastic, and each morning, when I come into the office and look at them, I acknowledge what I've accomplished.

But you know something? All of those awards don't help pay the bills one bit.

If you are a professional salesperson, you know how important it is to sell every single day. You know that all the awards and top achiever certificates in the world don't mean a thing if you aren't able to pay your bills. Making ends meet is the big prize.

We've already learned that prospecting is the key to your success. So let's take a look at what that really means by assembling a very simple form.

Across the top of a blank sheet of paper in your notebook, write down the following headings:

This form is part of a very simple program to monitor your calls. When you finish this book and begin your cold calling, you'll use the form for twenty-one straight days. When you've reached the twenty-first day, if you've used the form correctly, you'll have become much more successful at telephone prospecting.

Let me explain how each of these categories directly affects you. The very first column, "D," stands for the number of dials you make on any given day. Let's say, for example, that on a Monday, you step into the office, pick up the phone, and by the end of the day, reach a total of fifteen companies. You've made fifteen dials.

In other words, every time you hear someone answer the phone and say "Good morning, ABC Company,"—or anything that sounds vaguely similar—give yourself one tally under the "D" column. If, during the course of the day, you make two hundred calls but, due to busy signals, disconnected numbers, and fantastically bad luck, only hear one "Good morning, ABC Company," you get credit for that call only.

It's important to keep track of every dial that you make. Even if the person's next words after "Good morning, ABC Company," are "No sale, buddy!"—give yourself a tally.

The second column depends more on you. When you hear the secretary or switchboard operator—or anyone else— answer the phone, you're going to ask for a specific individual, either by name or by title. It might be the director of sales or the director of promotion. In any case, it's the person who can set the appointment for you. Every time you actually speak to a person who can give you an appointment, that's a completed call—"CC."

Don't panic! Whether or not they actually *give* you an appointment, once you speak to the right person, it's a completed call.

Each time your prospect talks to you, you're going to give him your best appointment-making pitch. (By the time you start keeping track with this form, you should have developed your own script and become quite familiar with it.) Every single time you give him the best approach you have and it results in an appointment, you're going to give yourself credit for that appointment in the "A" column.

The final columns, "V" and "S," keep track of your visits and sales. Of course, they don't necessarily reflect sales arising from the actual calls you made on a given day. Perhaps you spoke with someone two months ago and they didn't come through until this morning!

Here's a typical form reflecting one day's work:

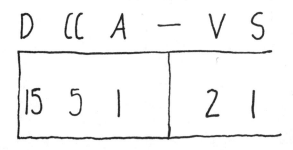

The first thing that most salespeople do after I've outlined this system is ask a lot of questions. "Suppose I get an answering machine? Suppose the prospect hangs up on me as soon as I start asking for an appointment? Suppose he hangs up before I even find out who I'm talking to?" Establish you own counting standards and stick to them. And remember, every time you make a dial it counts in your favor.

"In my favor? How can that possibly be? According to your numbers, Schiffman, I only talk to one person out of fifteen. How do fourteen rejections help me?"

With this question, we've come to the most difficult mental obstacle most salespeople ever encounter. Believe it or not, those fourteen rejections *do* help you. Here's how.

I'll use an actual example from a salesperson's work in my office—all I've done is round off the numbers for convenience. Over thirteen weeks this person posted the following figures:

D CC A — V S

300 150 50	50 5

Broken down for a single week, the numbers were as follows:

D CC A — V S

	D	CC	A	—	V	S
MON	12	6	1		1	0
TUE	10	5	2		2	1
WED	9	6	1		1	0
THU	10	4	1		0	0
FRI	15	6	0		1	0
TOTAL	56	27	5		5	1

At $6,000 commission per sale, his total personal revenue over thirteen weeks was $30,000. We can see in this example that every dial was really worth $100 to him—*even though he didn't get through!* Too simplistic? Not really. Think of it in reverse.

You know that in order for you to make five sales, you have to see fifty people. That's the ratio you've got to work with. How do you know? Your numbers tell you; and if you want to make money, you'll listen to them.

In order to see fifty people, you have to talk to 150 prospects and ask each one for an appointment.

In order to get 150 completed calls, you have to make 300 calls to begin with.

Therefore, every call is worth cash to you *as part of the cycle.* Without any one element of the cycle, you simply can't be successful.

Many salespeople instinctively understand this but are unable to put it in concrete terms. We just did. And you can use this system to your advantage by understanding—*and monitoring*—your success.

Let's say that you want to increase the amount of money that you make over the next thirteen weeks by $6,000. One more sale. If we follow the numbers that we've been working with, we see that you have to make a total of six sales. We know that you need to see fifty people to make five sales—but you goal now is to make six sales. Therefore, you have to increase your number of appointments from fifty people to sixty people. You have to take a look now at how many calls you originated in order to get the 50 appointments in the first place. That number is 300. So, for your purposes, 300=150=50. After some calculator work, you figure out that in order to get the ten additional appointments, you have to make a total of 180 completed calls, or a total of 360 initial dials, in order to reach your goal of six total sales over the thirteen weeks.

Here's another simple example. Your sales manager says he wants an increase of ten percent in your overall sales. You can begin by increasing the total number of dials that are made. If a ten percent increase requires 330 calls, you'd start there. Or, because you're getting better at this, you know that all you have to do is increase the total number of completed calls; so out of your 300 dials, you'll talk to 165 people instead of 150. Still a ten percent increase. Or you might find that your closing ratio could be improved: instead of closing five people out of fifty that you see in person, you might aim to close six—

and you'd become more aggressive at it once you understood the importance of that sale to your overall sales ratio.

The point I'm making is that by understanding your ratio and monitoring it with an ongoing method, you can be much more successful. Because you won't be groping around in the dark for "more sales," you'll know exactly what it takes for you (not the average salesperson, *you*) to get those sales.

Of course, all the appointments in the world won't help you if you can't close the sale. But the important point is that over-reliance on your product presentation skills can backfire. The key is to prospect, prospect, prospect: at your speed, using your goals, at your level.

A salesperson for a corporation my company was working with informed me that over a given period, she had made 94 dials that hadn't resulted in a single appointment—much less a sale. Not surprisingly, she didn't last long with the firm. But you know what we found out? She had never made the calls in the first place. It seemed as though she was spending as much time manufacturing numbers as trying to set up appointments. Here's the $64,000 question: who do you think she was fooling? The sales manager? Or herself?

❏ ❏ ❏ ❏

Since the purpose of this book is to help you make appointments, I won't go into great detail on the matter of making a presentation. However, I'm including some concise tips here on how best to use your time during this important part of the sales process.

After every appointment you go on, jot down some important facts about that appointment. Try to answer these questions: what was your objective? Did you meet it? What have you done to plan your follow-up work? When will that follow-up take place—next week, next month, next year?

Once you've answered these questions, file them away and integrate your plans into your calendar, or develop a simple tickler system. Be sure to remind yourself of key elements of the appointment and maybe some personal information about your prospect.

Recently, I conducted a survey and concluded that there were six primary factors behind a prospect's decision to purchase from a personal sales visit.

The prospects I polled were all unsolicited calls; that is to say, they had not initially perceived a need for the product or service until the salesperson contacted them through a cold call. Here's what I found out; I think the results will surprise you.

The most important factor in closing a prospect you've only contacted on the phone previously is your appearance in person. Without a doubt, the most important time you're going to have during your sales call are those first sixty seconds after you step in the door. First impressions really do count. The way you carry yourself in that crucial first minute will determine, more often than you'd expect, whether you will be successful that day. You *must* look and feel good. If you don't, you're doomed to failure.

Immediately following appearance is the handshake. Many people tend to think this isn't as important as it is. The prospect *likes* to feel that a salesperson is confident, and the handshake is an important indicator. A woman needs to shake hands in much the same way that a man does—firmly. If your hands get cold, stick them in your pocket to warm them up before you meet your prospect. (If you hands tend to perspire, there is a product on the market that will help alleviate that.) But whatever you do, reach out quickly and shake hands firmly and confidently.

The attitude and personal enthusiasm of the salesperson toward the product comes third. If you really believe in the product and your eyes light up as you talk about it, the prospect becomes more comfortable as you speak. Your enthusiasm and vocal presentation, of course, are also extremely important.

Your posture is also of value, and it's the fourth most important factor. It may not seem so crucial until you start to think about how you sit in a chair when you face an individual. If you slouch or are too rigid, it gives off "bad vibes" to the prospect. I've read all kinds of books about body language and non-verbal communication. The consensus is that thirty-five percent of our communication is verbal and the rest—sixty-five percent—is non-verbal. So think carefully about what you are "telling" your prospect when you slouch over in your chair or tense up like a pillar of granite. You've probably noticed yourself that the more relaxed the conversation gets (and the closer you get to the actual sale) the more relaxed and naturally alert you feel. Why not shoot for that same confident, professional approach throughout your presentation? And while you're at it, why not time your pauses more carefully and pull back to let your prospect talk every now and then? That shows you're interested in what he has to say. Good posture and personal bearing convey such things to the prospect quickly and effectively.

The speed of your voice, combined with your enthusiasm, ranks fifth. Of course, this ties in with your belief in the product. You must believe in the product and that must come through in measured, confident tones. Fast-talking salespeople often call to mind cliches of shysters nobody can trust. You've got nothing to hide. Take your time. Explain in detail why your product is great.

Ready for the shocker? The actual content of the presentation itself ranks *sixth* on the list. What does that tell you? The way you phrase the details is not as important as the way you present *yourself*. In fact, the skill with which you communicate your overall message may really be determined *the moment you walk in the office*. Not in the hours you spend setting up your charts and speeches.

Now, admittedly, if you don't know anything about your product and you stumble hopelessly through every appointment, you're probably not going to make a lot of sales. However, my studies show that if you are sincere about what you're doing, people are likely to accept the fact that you're a human being and keep listening if they come across a hitch in your presentation. In other words, even if you must say to the prospect, "I'm sorry, I made a mistake here," or "I honestly don't know the answer to that question," you're still more likely to get the sale than if you're smooth as glass and don't believe in the product in the first place.

As you can see, the actual words of the presentation are only one piece, and perhaps not the most important piece, of what is really going on in a sale. We know that presentation counts; but *don't overemphasize it*.

❏　❏　❏　❏

It's time to talk for a moment about the product.

A telephone system, a copier, a clock, a window, a carpet, furniture—all these have more in common than you might think. They each *fill consumer needs*. Once you identify those needs and point out to the right person how the item in question fills them, all products are identical.

Unfortunately, many salespeople overemphasize a product and fail to realize the reason somebody buys it: trust that's developed between the prospect and the salesperson. The prospect is confident that the salesperson can solve the problem at hand, that the salesperson's company can do the job it's promised to do.

The trick is, you've got to earn that trust during that all-important "get-acquainted" stage at the beginning of the whole process. You can spend all the time and money you want on developing fantastic presentations and having all kinds of flip charts printed up, but if you don't set up those first few minutes properly, you're going to fail.

Let's review what we've learned. In planning your sales strategy, we've seen that you must give top priority to prospecting effectively. Over-reliance on developing other areas, such as presentation, will shortchange you in a crucial area: making your first contacts with new leads.

More importantly, we've found out that by keeping an accurate record system of your prospecting, you can determine how effective you are as a salesperson every day.

Here's a good measure for you to use: if you see that you can't maintain 20-5-1 ratio (that is to say, twenty calls, five appointments, and one close), then you're probably doing something wrong. It could be that you're not strong enough in your sales presentation; or perhaps you're doing something wrong in the closing; or maybe you're not effective in making the calls in the first place. Worst of all, you might not be giving your prospecting efforts the proper amount of time.

Assess yourself if you see a problem. Be your own sales manager. As a professional salesperson, you must use your own numbers to determine how well you're doing. Once you generate real facts and real strategies to make more money, you'll agree that the method I've outlined is an effective way to answer your own question, "How'm I doing?"

In the next chapter, we'll be looking at ways to implement this strategy—and the other strategies in this book—into your sales work on a permanent basis.

CHAPTER NINE

The Perils of Reinventing the Wheel

When I first started in my sales career, I was convinced that I was going to be unlike any other salesperson who'd ever walked the earth. What did they have to teach me? I started out by not making any telephone calls. I went out each day, walked the streets, and expected people to throw business my way.

It didn't happen. I was leadless, and saw my prospects on an irregular basis at best, rejected simply because I never really *asked* them for anything except to "be in touch." Perhaps if I had taken advantage of some of the existing knowledge of sales techniques at my disposal, I would have gotten my career off to a better start.

You and I, as salespeople, don't need to reinvent the wheel. Instead, we need to practice solid sales techniques to be successful. To show you just how important this is, I'm going to tell you a very sad story.

❑   ❑   ❑   ❑

Recently, I conducted a program on phone prospecting at a large personnel agency in New York City. The people I was working with had been trained and retrained in their field (personnel placement) many times, with no lasting success. As I approached the podium on my first day, I had some trepidation—I knew that the approach I was about to recommend to them would require a significant change in their tactics. Shortly after I began to discuss the overall sales approach, a young woman (her name was Jill) raised her hand; I called on her.

"Mr. Schiffman," she said, "I've tried every technique in the world, including yours, and right now I'm involved in something very different from what you're describing. I'm not going to do this. I just don't think your system is going to work for me."

(As it turned out, she had never really tried my program. She may have found other programs that were similar, but not mine. More important, she hadn't been selling long enough to give *any* program a chance to work.)

I looked at her for a moment. I knew she was wrong. I walked over to her and said, "I want you to do me a favor. For the next twenty-one days I want you to follow the plan that I'm going to outline today. I want you to follow it religiously. Here's some inspiration." Before she could protest, I placed one half of a hundred dollar bill in her hand. I kept the other half; if she followed my instructions to the letter over the next weeks, she could obtain the other half of the bill from me—regardless of her results.

Before we go any further, I'll tell you right here that Jill got the $100 *and* became the star of the staff. What's so sad about that? Read on.

My arrangement with the company was quite simple. Every Wednesday at five, for three months, I came back. As the office closed down for the day, I would walk around and spend some time talking to the salespeople and going over problems.

The first week, nothing special happened. Then, on the second Wednesday after my initial presentation, I showed up a little early and saw quite a few people watching Jill use her script. By that time, Jill had done the things I had suggested—like buying a tape recorder and placing a mirror on her desk. As a result, she'd been making steady progress, and had, frankly, become something of an office sensation.

That afternoon, one of the salespeople, a young woman named Marcia, walked up to me and said, "Look what Jill's doing! She's reading a script, she's following all your procedures, and she's becoming *successful!*"

She kept raving about Jill's fantastic performance. "Steve," she said, "it's fantastic, she's doing just what you said; and it worked! I never thought it would actually *work.*"

Then I asked her, "Why don't you do it? How's your billing? Could you improve on what you're doing now?" (She was not doing well.)

"I can *always* stand to improve," said Marcia.

"So why don't you?"

There was a pause. Then she said, "Well, that wouldn't really work for me. But it sure is exciting to watch Jill go at it; I can tell you that much." And she walked away.

Isn't that a sad story?

❏ ❏ ❏ ❏

The point here is that each of us can do what the star of the staff does. It requires no special talent to make telephone calls in a persistent manner using a script, a mirror, a timer, and perhaps a tape recorder. Honest. It requires no mysterious talent to become successful. All that's required is consistency and the willingness to become your own manager.

I'll give you another example. While working with a real estate company, I calculated that a particular salesperson named John made something in the neighborhood of fifteen dollars an hour based on a full eight-hour day. (You can figure out your own hourly rate pretty easily, even if you're on straight commission. Take the number of hours that you work daily; usually nine hours a day is about right when you consider all down time. Multiply that by the number of days a year you work. Now, use that figure and divide it into the total amount of money you made last year. That gives you an average hourly figure. Once you realize how much your time is worth to you, you become very enthusiastic about productivity.) John said to me, "I make ten calls a day, Steve; I get five appointments from those calls, and from those appointments I'm able to close a sale. I'm doing fantastically on my ratios—but I want to increase my sales. What do I do?"

Here's what I told him: "Let's do this, John: why not increase your calls by one, every day?"

"One call a day?" he asked. "That won't get me anywhere."

"Well," I said, "can you make ten more calls a day?"

"Nope."

"How about one, then?"

"Sure, I can *make* one," John said, a little impatient with me, "but I can tell you right now it won't do a thing for my paycheck."

"Let's check that out," I said, reaching for the calculator on his desk.

By this point you should be able to guess what we found out. If John made just one more call a day, that would be five calls a week: an extra morning's work. If he did that every single week, four weeks a month, he'd be making at least twenty more calls a month. If his ratio remained high (and one more call a day probably wouldn't throw him off too much) that's two more sales, or in his case, $10,000 in commissions. He made that extra call every day.

Do you know your numbers? Do you know how many calls it takes for you to make a sale? If you do, then you can determine how much money you're going to make each and every year. How? By setting up a plan with realistic goals and sticking to it. By realizing the number of telephone calls you'll need, the number of appointments you should make, and the number of sales that you're guaranteeing yourself to close each year.

Why don't more salespeople do this?

❏ ❏ ❏ ❏

By buying this book you've demonstrated that you're a motivated individual. That was the first step in a long series of steps guaranteeing your success. Used properly, this book will help you. Used inconsistently, without a willingness to stick to your own personal plan, it won't get you anywhere. Which works out better for you? You'd think the answer would be an easy one, but many salespeople have a lot of difficulty on this point.

Let's take the question even further. Why do salespeople fail?

One big reason is that they often try to reinvent the wheel. Instead of going with a system that works, they "think on their feet." And lose sales.

I started this book by telling you that there is no easy way to sell. There is, however, an easy way to categorize the different ways salespeople find to fail. It's a simple acronym, one that says everything you need to know on the subject. I'd like you to jot it down in your notebook now. It is:

F. U. D. H.

The "F" stands for Fear. If, after buying this book, you brought it back and said to a fellow salesperson, "Hey, I think this book can help me out," he might respond with, "It won't work." And as far as that person's concerned, I have to admit, it won't. What about you, though? Remember, this book can never work for the person who's scared to try something new.

The fear of others constantly stops us in our tracks. We're afraid of what other people will say to us. We're afraid of the competition. And we're afraid of rejection. Virtually every salesperson I talk to tells me that rejection is at the top of the charts when it comes to fear. Let's be frank: rejection is scary. And I can't minimize that for you. The fear of the negative reaction from a new prospect is an inherent part of selling, one that you must face in your role as a professional finder and solver of business problems. You're going to have to initiate constant contact with a great many individuals, most of whom really don't care whether you make your next mortgage payment. The only thing you can do to deal with rejection is face it head on. It's part of the game; and if you keep track of the "no's," you realize that all they really do is introduce you to another "yes."

The "U" stands for Uncertainty, not only about the outcome of a particular sales effort, but also about life goals. I don't know whether people are more afraid of success or failure. When I think of some of the salespeople I've encountered over the years, I find myself asking some tough questions. Did they really want to succeed? Or were they worried somehow about what might happen if they actually hit that quota? Were they involved in an elaborate scheme that looked promising for a while, but had as its real goal self-punishment? Don't laugh. I've seen many salespeople get so worked up about so many areas *other* than selling that they honestly seemed to me to force failure on themselves—or, more accurately, prevent their own success.

Many salespeople are uncertain about their desire for success. They think success is too simple, that there must be a catch somewhere. Illustrate a simple formula, show that success can be achieved in a relatively simple manner, and watch as their faces change and fear spreads throughout their bodies. When it comes right down to it, many are unable to commit to success.

The "D" stands for Doubt: the kind of self-doubt that we all face. Even those of us who appear incredibly self-assured or even egotistical have a degree of self-doubt. In sales, this is often magnified. There is some element of risk to every idea, and as a salesperson, one is basically engaged in turning unrealized ideas into action. That takes confidence but also breeds insecurity. If we don't strengthen ourselves with practice against this anxiety over our performance, we begin a cycle. And it starts, innocently enough, with nothing.

For many, it begins with an uneasy feeling about the results of the day's phone work. A salesperson may decide, as a result, to "lay off for a while." He stops making calls. The next morning, he realizes he's behind in his prospecting, and begins to think (illogically) that this somehow supports his earlier feeling that "something was wrong" with him. So he can't get a good start on the day's calls. Non-action creates self-doubt. He's going nowhere in circles. He sees it all happening and his confidence falls further. He doesn't know what to do anymore. He's paralyzed.

How do I know all this about doubt? Believe me, I'm no stranger to the cycle I've just described. Now and then, when I pick up the telephone or have to show up for a crucial appointment or seminar, I freeze up. Suppose I forget the opening line of my speech. Suppose I catch laryngitis while I'm driving. Suppose the car breaks down. Suppose when I get there, the room is completely empty. Each "suppose" creates more self-doubt. But, lo and behold, I arrive safely, I walk onstage, and when I start, it all disappears as though there had never been any doubt at all.

The secret is to plunge ahead to take the first step. The first time you tried to ice-skate, ride a horse, water-ski—almost any new and exciting activity—you had your doubts. And you probably fell. But you got up again. Then you took the next step; and you practiced that next step, until finally you got it right. But what you really did was give yourself confidence; you removed the anxiety by taking the initial step. All salespeople need to take the first step in order to remove the doubt.

The final letter, "H," stands for Habits. There's nothing wrong with habits in and of themselves. Habits enable us to function. When you get up in the morning, you don't *think* about whether you brush your teeth up-and-down or left-to-right; or whether you put your right shoe on before your left one; or whether you lock the door as you leave the house. You do these things automatically. They've become habits, ones you've put to good use as a self-sufficient person. *Bad* habits are the ones we want to break.

The average bad habit takes between five and twenty-one days to break. That means if you ever want to stop biting your nails, scratching your hair, or leaving the cap off the toothpaste, it's not going to happen overnight. You have to be conscious of it every day until finally you no longer do it. In fact, you have to develop a habit of *not* doing it.

In order to break bad habits, the first thing you have to do is identify which ones they are. If you want to acquire good habits, you have to determine which habits you want to develop and decide to work on them. The consistency you manage to bring to both sides of that equation will determine your success; and you should keep in mind that the bulk of your work will have to be done during these first crucial weeks.

Don't keep track of your calls for two days, decide it's pointless, and then give up. It's been proven: the wheel already exists. Learn to use it. Don't try to reinvent it. It will take between five and twenty-one days of *real* effort on your part to get into the habit of becoming successful, the habit of making quality prospecting calls every single day.

Once you've done that, you'll be ready for the real challenge: your competition. In the next chapter, we'll be taking a look at the battles you'll have to wage in order to achieve—and maintain—success as a professional salesperson.

CHAPTER TEN

Business as War

At one point in my presentation, I point out that there is a fine line between war and business. Inevitably, audience members nod their heads in agreement. When I ask them to list some of the parallels between war and business, the crowd can get quite enthusiastic, as example after example is shouted out. Here are some of the most common features, according to my audiences, that war and business share:

- Ammunition
- Strategy
- Captains
- Leaders
- Life
- Death
- Success
- Failure
- Goals
- Tactics
- Winners
- Losers

As you might guess, the list goes on and on.

In wartime, of course, it's easy to understand the necessity of having well-trained troops. I can't think of anyone who'd be excited about skipping his basic training, piling into an airplane, taking a rifle in hand, and rushing onto the battlefield hoping to carry out the simple order of "fighting the enemy." Yet all too often, we go out each day as salespeople and fail to accept the necessity of planning, strategizing, and, yes, even undergoing a little "basic training."

It's true. You're fighting a war every day that you sell. In this chapter, we're going to concentrate on how best to prepare for battle. What ammunition should you carry? How do you prepare to charge? Do you know when to retreat? What role do the spies play? How about the generals? Most important, have you trained yourself properly?

❑   ❑   ❑   ❑

Let's look at the role of the spy in wartime. A spy performs an important function for his army. 2,000 years ago, a great Chinese general said that there was nothing more valuable than understanding what the competition was going to do before they did it. If there's a way to accomplish this effectively without spies, no one's come up with it yet.

You need to accept the fact that there is competition out there, real companies with real salespeople, and that they are trying, much like you, to undercut their business rivals. As a salesperson, you need to know what your competition is saying when they call for this appointment, and how it differs from what you're saying. As you may have already gathered, you can prepare yourself most effectively for whatever objections may come your way by understanding where they come from. When the objection has to do with your competition, you should listen especially carefully.

In a real way, then, there is a little bit of the spy in every good salesperson. He or she is looking constantly to see what the competition's doing. We've already seen that there are very few people you can't get through to by mentioning *their* competition—now what about *yours*?

Start to look at ways in which you can find out more about your opposite number in the business world. If you work for XYZ Widget Corporation, there are things that you *must* find out about Widgets International, which wants your customers. Specifically, you should know:

1. Their products.
2. Their prices.
3. The customers they target (their market).
4. The percentage of the market they control.
5. How many salespeople they have in a territory.
6. How much of a discount they're giving.
7. How they're selling.
8. What they're saying about you and your product.
9. What they say when your customers won't switch.
10. The comparisons they make between your firms.

This information is your ammunition. Since you'll know upfront exactly what the competition is saying about you, you'll be able to handle it more effectively in your telephone calls. If the competition is truly aggressive (and make no mistake, much of it is), then you're prepared for that aggressiveness and can try to turn it around in a positive way.

Well. While you're working so hard as a spy, what's going on at headquarters? What are the generals doing? And what *is* the role of the top brass, anyway?

Obviously, in your army, not everyone's a general. There's probably a fair sprinkling of captains, too. Usually, the general is the owner of the company, or CEO, or president, or some other bigwig you probably don't see that much (unless you're working in a smaller operation). Usually, the captain that *you* deal with is your sales manager. And what exactly is the role of the sales manager in today's sales force? The answer is a complicated one.

The sales forces of today are more sophisticated than they once were. Motivated salespeople (like you) have a better understanding of the way they are going to sell, and the "captain" may or may not know that. Many sales managers, when asked what they want their salespeople to do, respond by saying, "I want them to sell."

Actually, that's not what they want. They really want them to *prospect* and to make effective telephone calls.

And as far as you're concerned, your sales manager's role is really minimal. Stop and think about it. The sales manager's role *should* be to approve your commission check and hand it to you on payday. It should *not* be his role to motivate you.

Many salespeople wait for the sales manager to tell them to sell. That's unnecessary! If you've been following the procedures I've outlined so far, you won't *need* to have someone set a goal for you. You'll know how to determine what you're going to do to be successful six months from now. There's no surprise element. Any good salesperson knows his or her success depends on personal prospecting and the goals that arise from it. To have a sales manager walk up to your desk and tell you solemnly, "Peter, I think it's time for you to pick up your sales," is *ridiculous*. Not only should you know before the sales manager does that you need to pick up your sales—you should know *how* you're going to pick up your sales.

You might be asking yourself at this point, "Well, then, what is the role of a sales manager? What's he supposed to be doing for me?" The answer is a simple one. *Nothing.*

The sales manager is really just a conduit between you and management. He or she should be open and give you the opportunity to talk freely about what's happening in the field; that's important information that should be conveyed to top management. But you should not ask the sales manager for more than that. Below are some jobs that the sales manager must never be counted on to do:

Finding and developing leads

Providing motivation

Offering help (other than in closing)

Getting appointments

Telling you what you're doing right

Telling you what you're doing wrong

Lending moral support

Extending sympathy

Taking on the role of a mother

Now that we've established what the sales manager is there for, let's move up our ladder. What should the generals be doing?

The generals in your army should be planning and forming strategy that makes full use of the "intelligence" you've gathered in the course of your sales work. In other words, if your "orders" are to head out to sell the new Model One

Widget, and you can't move the item at all because there's no market for it, you'd better high-tail it back to your captain. He, in turn, had better high-tail it back to his general, so that the mistake in strategy can be corrected—quick.

If, on the other hand, the Model One is doing fantastically, and the sales are really rolling in for you, that kind of information should make it up to the general, too. (Presumably you won't have to try too hard; he should realize what's happening when he signs your commission check.)

So that's really the general's job—to determine the strategy and use all the information you give him to set up ways of selling the product more effectively. Beyond that, though, there's not much he can do. (Bear in mind that with the exception of those of the Israeli army, very few real generals actually make it out onto the battlefields. It should come as no surprise, then, that when you're out on the firing line, you're on your own.)

If the general has made a mistake, you can blame him all you want, but the fact is your commission check is still going to be affected by his or her decisions tomorrow morning. Most enlightened companies today realize how important it is to get feedback from their salespeople, and look forward to discussing the issues that come up from day to day with them. However, many small companies really don't want to hear what the salesperson has to say. And that's too bad.

If you should find yourself in the unfortunate situation of having no access whatsoever to the general (and by that I mean not even indirect access through a captain), then you have two choices in front of you. One, you can create the access. Two, you can go find another army to fight for. If the communication is that bad and doesn't show much promise of changing in the near future, the only thing that's going to happen is that you're going to lose. That's called death.

In sales, there are real casualties when people lose. Losing means not making any money. You can't afford to die—nor can you afford not to make any money. If you find that your product is not selling, and you are doing everything in your power that you're supposed to do, then tell the general right away. If he can't or won't listen, avoid a bloodbath and waste no time in getting out.

Now, let's take a look at training and how that affects you. As it happens, the soldiers who've been most successful through the centuries have been the ones with the best training. Virtually every victory in the history of human warfare was backed up by trained soldiers who understood what their mission was and knew how to carry it out.

Much the same is true of victories in the business world. Your training will determine your success. It must be constant training, the kind that requires you to upgrade yourself and your knowledge of your product, its market, and its competition, each and every day. If you get fat and flabby, you'll fail.

You have to look at yourself each day when you put on your uniform (your business suit) take up your armaments (your briefcase and business card), and gather your ammunition (your presentation tools and knowledge of the selling environment). You have to like what you see.

When you make your calls, be prepared to give yourself a little boost if you feel your initiative failing. Learning how to keep up your morale is part of your training, too.

Don't start the war unprepared. Know how to use what you bring to the battlefield. That slight nervousness you feel is natural—after all, you're going to war. Use it. Don't let it get in the way of what you're doing.

Keep your weapons clean and well-organized. I'm referring, of course, to your briefcase. Don't carry around a lot of junk. There's nothing more humiliating than opening up your briefcase in the middle of a presentation and having a banana peel, last week's newspaper, and an empty vitamin bottle fall out onto the prospect's rug.

Dress sharp. You have a uniform: it's a business suit. Remember that you're wearing it for a reason; it should give you a measure of pride in your appearance and should also mark you as a professional. Project that pride and professionalism in your calls. (And keep an eye on those folks in your office who dress "casually." You notice how they never seem to close enough sales? There's a reason. They're not there for business.)

Concentrate on your assignment. Stop whatever else you're doing and concentrate on winning the war. Don't do two things at once (for example, pitching one prospect and writing down notes about another one); you're bound to mess one of them up. Just do your job.

❑   ❑   ❑   ❑

Another fascinating thing about wars and the generals who wage them is the matter of belief in a cause. Robert E. Lee and Ulysses S. Grant each deeply believed that his efforts were justly undertaken. Each understood the necessity of instilling in his men that same sense of working toward the correct goal, of having a reason for winning.

Do you feel it?

You need to be committed to your cause: your company, your family, your pocketbook. However you identify it, if you are not convinced that you're doing the right thing, if you can't quite see the benefit of solving people's problems with your product, if you really don't think your company's efforts are for the best—then you may have some difficulty in succeeding.

CONCLUSION

The Lemonade Stand

Cold calling is not the most glamorous part of a business's day-to-day activities. It's grunt work and, to make matters worse, it's scary. If you could get someone else to make the calls, you probably would. (In fact, so would I!) The fact is, few, if any, salespeople actually *enjoy* the cold calling process.

It follows that its popularity, if not its necessity, is limited. Most people don't want to do what they "have to do"—they'd rather focus on the things they get a kick out of. Personally, I like selling. I enjoy the one-on-one contact that I have in an appointment. But (isn't there always a "but" right about this time?) I can't get in the door without making the calls. And neither can you.

When I first started to introduce the concept of shooting for a specific ratio based on one's statistics (I call it "20-5-1" for short), people told me it was too simplistic. My response was to ask if they had a better method. So far, nobody's come up with one.

❑ ❑ ❑ ❑

I once had a sales trainer tell me that all that was necessary to succeed was learning how to sell; the appointments, he promised, would take care of themselves. I'd love to be able to tell you that he was fired for spreading such garbage, but the truth is more complicated. He's still out there teaching. His course sounds like Psych 101, and probably offers about as much practical sales guidance to his trainees. Watch out for him and others like him.

If you are going to really sell—and by that I mean make big money—you're eventually going to learn to make cold calls. The techniques outlined in the previous chapters are the keys to your success. As you follow the steps I've outlined in this book, there are some questions you should be asking yourself to be sure that you're getting the most out of your efforts. Here they are:

Who will you be calling?

How did you generate your list of suspects? (Note that I didn't say "prospect." A suspect is someone you haven't talked to yet.) Be sure to allocate enough time in your weekly schedule to maintain a good base of leads.

What is your approach?

Remember, your goal is not to sell over the phone. Set the appointment. Keep the rejection factor in mind. Especially at the beginning of the process, maintain a sense of perspective. Know that it will take a certain number of calls for you to get an appointment. Be prepared to make the calls that will yield the results you desire. Don't panic; be a professional.

In most sales organizations, twenty calls are necessary to set five appointments. If your goal next week is to set six appointments, you should know that you'll need to make more calls. Understanding *your* individual rejection rate (or IRR) will help you remain relatively calm during those first few hang - ups you encounter.

As to your scripts, you should refine them to your own individual needs. While I've included model scripts at the end of this book, you shouldn't use them word-for-word; use *your* script word-for-word. And if you find that you're not getting a satisfactory number of appointments, start reworking your script. Your approach can be either hard or soft, depending upon you and your lists of suspects. But you must be positive. You must get the appointment by asking for it—not by waiting to see what the person on the other end of the line will do.

At a recent banking seminar, the issue of cold calling happened to come up. The bankers expressed some hesitation at the suggestion that they call any "total strangers" at all, and one young man mentioned that he'd tried cold calling, but felt "funny" when he asked a prospect for an appointment. The instructor asked him how many times someone had walked into a bank with $100,000, asking to buy a CD. "Once," was the young man's reply. "What happened?" asked the instructor. Of course, the young banker recalled every detail of the transaction. The trainer smiled. His point was that the sale that "lands in your lap" does occur—but so infrequently that it stands out like a sore thumb. Do you want your sales to be that rare? Wouldn't you rather have so many that you have to consult your notebook for details?

Are you placing the proper emphasis on your prospecting efforts?

Don't fall into the trap of "closing more sales" at the expense of your prospecting.

Think of the first thing you ever sold in your life. Chances are, your first business venture was a corner lemonade stand— it was for my kids. One weekend, they took a large can of frozen lemonade, mixed it with water in a pitcher, and walked outside. There they set up a table, a chair, and a sign that said "LEMONADE—TWENTY-FIVE CENTS." For the first hour, nobody walked by. The proprietors thought seriously about drinking their inventory, but realized that if they drank it all, they'd have nothing to sell. Finally, a person strolled by, and the kids thought they had a sale. But the person merely stopped, looked at the sign, smiled, and continued walking.

So it went through the day. One after another, with big lulls between their visits, prospects walked past the stand. It was the fifth person to pass them who actually stepped up and bought a cup of lemonade. By the end of the day, the kids had learned that based on total sales of four cups of lemonade, they could expect roughly two thirds of their prospects to turn them down.

The next day, as they were preparing to begin the process once again, my youngest came up with a brilliant idea.

"Why don't we try a different corner? One with more people?" she asked. I'd been eavesdropping; when I heard this I asked her to explain her suggestion. "Well, Dad," she began patiently, "there were only twelve people who walked by our stand yesterday, and most of the time we just sat around. We only sold four cups all day long. Now, if we find a corner where a hundred people will pass us, we'll sell a lot more lemonade."

There is a special moment in the lives of certain parents, a moment when they realize that their child is a genius.

Maybe I'm letting my pride get the better of me, though. Maybe we all know what my daughter explained to me. Maybe it's common knowledge that if you get in front of more people, you're apt to make more sales. Then again, maybe not.

Of course, you don't *have* to put any time into your prospecting. If your objective is to sell a pencil, you could conceivably stand in a store window and wait for the people walking by to see that you're holding pencils in your hand and take it into their heads to walk in the door and ask you if you'd mind selling one to them. The only problem is, you wouldn't be a salesperson anymore. You'd be what's called a "retailer."

Now, in one sense, you, as an outside salesperson, *do* have quite a bit in common with the retailer, whose three most important assets, as you've probably heard, are location, location, and location. You have to make your *own* location. But not by finding a good street corner. The *telephone* is the way you create that location, by constantly calling individuals whom you suspect are in need of your service. If you do this in a manner that you know works for you, every day, you will, in my daughter's terms, sell a lot of lemonade.

Are you acting as your own sales manager?

If so, you can consider yourself a staff unto yourself. Once you do, you're responsible for making sure that your staff: calls every day; uses the script; avoids reinventing the wheel; and keeps accurate records and personal statistics. You also have to: set your goals; keep on top of the competition; plan your strategy; and adjust your plans to take unforeseen factors into account.

When I first started making sales calls, my wife and I sat at the kitchen table with a tape recorder. She acted as my prospect; I worked from a written script. As we practiced, I taped each and every "call," and finally used the material on the tapes to refine my sales strategy and rewrite my script.

Listening to each and every call was time-consuming, no doubt about it. It would sometimes take hours to perfect my approach, but I had no choice. I had to set and close my appointments! I was in business for myself and without sales; I couldn't afford to make mistakes with actual prospects. Only after ironing everything out could I approach real, live businesspeople.

Try it. Collar someone and make him treat you in exactly the same way a tough prospect would on the phone. Tape what you say to one another. By listening to a hundred telephone calls, you're going to see that certain objections come up again and again. Prepare for them. Make sure you put in a good effort at turning the most common ones around *without even thinking about it*. Know exactly what you have to say and be ready to say it.

How do you motivate yourself?

Whether it's a photograph of your dream house, an ad for a sports car, or just a figure scrawled on a piece of paper, tack something onto the wall that reminds you of why you're doing what you're doing. Look at it every day.

Use your imagination. If you need to run around the block in order to get excited, do it. If you need to sing at the top of your lungs to warm your voice up, do it. If you need to look at your children every morning and picture the education you'd like to be able to offer them, do it. Whatever is necessary for you to motivate yourself, don't be afraid to give it a try.

You don't have to be flamboyant, either. Read motivational books, listen to sales-related tapes. Set aside a time during the day when you drop everything, gather your resources, and give yourself a little pep talk. Most important, think positively every single day.

❏ ❏ ❏ ❏

Here again is the guarantee I mentioned earlier.

If, after reading this book, you don't agree that it's the best one on the market in the area of appointment making through cold calls, contact me and I'll return your money without question. All I ask is that you supply me with the completed notebook and script development materials used over the same time, and the call sheets recording the number of calls you made over the weeks and their results.

If you do this, and enclose a note expressing your displeasure with your results, I'll write you a check for the full purchase price of the book. The fact is, though, it's absolutely, positively impossible to fail with my method—if you only try.

In my office, we have regular sales meetings, but they're a little different in one respect from the meetings in many offices. Certainly you've heard the expression, "Have a nice day." Where I work, we don't say that; we say, "Make it a productive day." It reminds us that we're in control of our destiny, that our success or our failure is in our own hands. It's just the same with you.

Make it a productive day!

Sample Scripts

Finally—you're ready to begin.

Almost every product that you buy today has a set of instructions; many even state something along the lines of "use only as directed." I take a slightly different approach on the matter of tinkering with these scripts. Certainly you should feel free to adapt them to your own personal style. But do so in keeping with the spirit of the program outlined in the preceding chapters. Don't overembellish.

As you look these scripts over, they may seem a little ambitious. They're meant to be. They're simple, and they're direct. That's why they work.

At one of my seminars recently, a group of salespeople expressed some reservations about these scripts. Why were they so aggressive? Where were the probing questions? How were they to "draw the prospects in?"

Their problem, of course, was that they were wasting their time talking to people they should have classified as simple rejections in the first minute of the conversation. And anyway, actually selling over the phone, as I've mentioned earlier, is *not* what cold calling is about.

To address the concerns these people raised, I decided to try a little experiment. I sat down one Tuesday and made seven cold calls in a two-hour period. I got through to two people and got one appointment *by using the scripts reproduced below—word for word.* That's fifty percent. I asked the sales manager if he could match that figure using his current methods. He couldn't. When the salespeople finally saw the results of the program, they decided to give it a try.

The salespeople I'm discussing were lucky. They kept an open mind. If you do the same thing, you'll see a marked improvement in your performance.

The scripts outlined here are the basis for the work you're about to undertake. Obviously, as you get more proficient at it, you'll change a word here and there to fit your own style and needs. But the same approach applies—and that's the point. You'll stop wasting time by having extended conversations on the phone. You'll be direct in asking for the appointment. You'll know what you're going to say in advance.

When I start my seminars, I usually begin with the sentence, "When God wanted to punish salespeople, He invented the cold call." That actually sums up my feelings, and possibly yours as well, about the cold call. You, and only you, can reverse the "curse" and turn it into an opportunity—by beginning to use the techniques outlined in earlier chapters and the scripts provided here.

Initial Contact Script

Good morning _____ this is
_____ from _____. The reason
I'm calling is to tell you about our new
_____ program which can effectively increase the productivity of _____. Mr.
_____ I'm sure that you like other people
want to have an effective _____.

Follow-up Script

Good morning _____ this is
_____ from _____. A number of
weeks ago I contacted you, and you asked me to call
you back today to set up an appointment. Would
_____ be good for you?

Third Party Endorsement Script

Good morning _____ this is
_____ from _____. The reason
I'm call you is I'm the _____ of
_____ and we've just completed working
on a major program for _____ which was
extremely successful in increasing _____.
What I'd like to do _____ is stop by next
_____ to tell you about the success I had
at _____.

Referral Script

Good morning _____ this is
_____ from _____. Let me tell
you why I'm calling you. The other day I was
meeting with _____ at _____
and we were discussing a number of projects that we
had just completed for the _____. He said
that I should really contact you as you are absolutely
the right person to talk to about some of the programs
that we have been doing. Can we get together? How
about _____ at _____?

Examples of pitch with built-in "yes" question:

Insurance: Hello, Mr./Mrs. _____, this is
_____ from _____ here in
_____. Mr./Mrs. _____, are
you interested in increasing your coverage to protect
your family against illness or accident? That's great,
then we should get together. How about
_____ at _____?

Hard Goods: Good morning, Mr./Mrs.
_____, this is _____ from
_____ here in _____. I'm calling today to introduce you to our new
_____—which can effectively increase
your production. Are you interested in increasing
your production there? Good. Can we get together?
How does _____ at _____
sound?

Real Estate: Good morning, Mr./Mrs.
_____. This is _____ from
_____. Mr./Mrs. _____, are
you interested in having your house listed on the
market and receiving a high price for it? Good! Then
we should get together. How's _____ at
_____?

Examples of pitch without built-in "yes" question?

Personnel: Good morning, Mr./Mrs.

_____, this is _____ from _____ here in _____. We've just completed a major staffing program for a large Fortune 500 company which has allowed them to save substantial money on temporary services. I'd like to stop by and tell you about some of the successes that we've been having with these kinds of companies. Can we get together? How about _____ at _____?

Automobiles: Good morning, Mr./Mrs.

_____, this is _____ from _____ here in _____. Mr./Mrs. _____, we've just been able to put together a complete financing package which has helped many people to own our fine automobiles. I'd like to stop by to show you some of the success that we've been having with these automobile packages. Would _____ at _____ be good?

Also by Stephan Schiffman:

Closing Techniques (That Really Work!)
Trade paperback, 160 pages, $7.95; ISBN: 1-55850-410-9

Simple, effective techniques for making the sale, from America's #1 corporate sales trainer. Contains tested advice, sample scenarios, and scripts—everything you need to improve your closing skills.

Cold Calling Techniques (That Really Work!)
Trade paperback, 152 pages, $7.95; ISBN: 1-55850-860-0

Proven advice on the most difficult selling situations. Schiffman shows you how to craft your message, how to deal with secretaries or assistants, how to catch a prospect's interest and attention, and how to turn a cold call into a sale.

The 25 Sales Habits of Highly Successful Salespeople, 2nd Edition
Trade paperback, 128 pages, $5.95; ISBN: 1-55850-391-9

Demonstrates how most successful salespeople practice powerful, effective sales techniques—and shows you how to make these techniques part of your own set of selling skills. From tips on developing selling plans to strategies for getting quality referrals, Schiffman's advice can help you sell more.

The 25 Most Common Sales Mistakes
(and How to Avoid Them), 2nd Edition
Trade paperback, 128 pages, $6.95; ISBN: 1-55850-511-3

Take the negatives and make them positives with Schiffman's advice: not being obsessed, not taking notes, not taking the prospective's point of view, and more.

The Consultant's Handbook
Trade paperback, 252 pages, $12.95; ISBN: 0-937860-93-X

Everything you need to know to start a lucrative consulting business. Detailed information on finding clients, making successful presentations, pricing your services, collecting receivables, and even saving money on taxes.

Power Sales Presentations
Trade paperback, 192 pages, $7.95; ISBN: 1-55850-252-1

A step-by-step guide to preparing and delivering powerful sales presentations. Includes examples of real-life dialogues that show you not just what to say, but how to respond to a prospect's questions or comments.

If you cannot find these titles at your favorite retail outlet, you may order them directly from the publisher. BY PHONE: Call 1-800-872-5627 (in Massachusetts 617-767-8100). We accept Visa, Mastercard, and American Express. $4.50 will be added to your total order for shipping and handling. BY MAIL: Write out the full title of the books you'd like to order and send payment, including $4.50 for shipping and handling to: Adams Publishing, 260 Center Street, Holbrook, MA 02343. 30-day money-back guarantee.